"To laugh often and love much..
to appreciate beauty, to find the best in others,
to give one's self...
this is to have succeeded."
Ralph Waldo Emerson

This book is dedicated to my wife Carole,
without whom there would be no success.

"I'm here from the government, and I am here to help you."
For some people that phrase instills confidence that the
government of the people, for the people, and by the people
has come to the rescue of its citizenry and will be providing
assistance in some important matter. For other people that
phrase instills a fear that when the government gets involved,
things tend to get overly complicated and complex. When it
comes to retirement planning, both mindsets are right.

Although sometimes it may seem like the purpose of tax laws is
to merely take as much of our hard earned money as possible, tax
laws are also written to encourage certain activities and discourage
others. The tax deduction for mortgage interest is an example of
Congress' attempt to encourage and facilitate home ownership.
And so it is with retirement planning.

In an effort to encourage us to save for our own retirement rather
than be dependent upon the government and programs like Social
Security, Congress has passed laws providing opportunities for
us to save for our own retirement while also reducing our income
tax burden—a definite win-win situation for us. Perhaps the most
popular and most effective ways of saving for your retirement
are through IRAs and 401(k)s. More than 3 ½ trillion dollars are
invested in IRAs while 401(k)s hold investments worth another
3 trillion dollars.

When it comes to planning for your retirement, IRAs and 401(k)s
offer tremendous opportunities, but also pitfalls and traps for
the unwary. As with any government-created program, there is a
veritable avalanche of rules that can be viewed by pessimists as
being stifling complications filled with financial danger. To the
optimist, however, these rules provide opportunities for you to
adopt IRA and 401(k) strategies specifically tailored to yours and
your family's needs—not just for now, but for the next generation.

That is where this book comes in. This book may not turn you
into an optimist if that is not your predisposition, but it will provide
you with the truth about all the ins and outs, the regulations, and

the loopholes involved with IRAs and 401(k)s. It will help you identify both the pitfalls and the opportunities. It will help you help yourself toward a secure retirement.

"The question isn't at what age I want to retire, it's at what income." George Foreman

TRUTH

IRA

Although it may seem like the purpose of tax laws is merely to confiscate as much of our money as possible, tax laws are written by legislators to encourage and discourage particular activities. The tax deduction for mortgage interest is an example of Congress' attempt to encourage and facilitate homeownership. And so it is with retirement planning.

In an effort to encourage us to save for our own retirement rather than depend on the government and programs like Social Security, Congress has passed laws providing opportunities for us to save for our own retirement in a tax-advantaged way. Perhaps the two best ways to do this for most people are the IRA and the 401(k). When it comes to retirement planning, the IRA offers tremendous opportunities. As always, there is a veritable avalanche of rules that can be viewed by pessimists as stifling complications. However, to the optimist, these rules present opportunities to help you adapt an IRA strategy that will work best for you and your family.

IRA is an acronym for Individual Retirement Account. It comes in the form of the traditional IRA (if anything that has only been around since 1974 can be referred to as traditional) and the Roth IRA, named after its primary Congressional proponent, Delaware Senator William Roth. The traditional IRA was originally intended to provide a means for people who were not covered by company pensions to be able to save for their own retirement in a tax-advantaged manner. In 1981, Congress broadened the availability of IRAs to all workers regardless of whether they were covered by a company pension.

> When it comes to retirement planning, the IRA offers tremendous opportunities.

The Roth IRA became law in 1997. Two years prior to its enactment, a similar proposal entitled the American Dream Savings Account was passed by Congress but vetoed by then-President Clinton. Apparently, they did not share the same dream. The Roth IRA was the crowning achievement of the legislative career of Senator William Roth, who a scant three years after the passage of the legislation was sent into his own retirement when he lost his bid for reelection to the Senate.

With a traditional IRA, contributions to the IRA are often tax deductible and accumulate income on a tax-deferred basis. With a Roth IRA, you pay income tax on the money you put into the IRA. However, the money grows untaxed, and you are able to take money out of a Roth IRA free of all income taxes.

Traditional IRA

A traditional IRA is a retirement account into which the law permits you to make, in many cases, tax-deductible contributions on an annual basis of as much as $5,000. For those of you reaching the age of 50, not only do you get a birthday card from AARP (and how do they always manage to know when everyone's 50th birthday is?), but also you are permitted by law to contribute an extra $1,000 to your IRA, for an annual total of $6,000. Beginning in 2009, the amount of the annual contributions are adjusted annually for inflation, in $500 increments.

Perhaps the major requirement for eligibility for any IRA is earned income. However, there are limitations on the amount of income you may have to qualify for a Roth IRA. There is no limitation on the amount of income you are permitted to earn to be eligible for a traditional IRA. In addition, you must be under the age of 70 1/2 to contribute to an IRA, but more on that later.

If you are married and neither you nor your spouse has a retirement plan at work, your contributions to your traditional IRAs will be fully tax deductible in that year. Even if you do have a retirement plan at work, you may be able to deduct some or even all of your IRA contributions if your taxable income meets certain guidelines. For 2008, the guidelines were particularly restrictive for married people filing separate income tax returns. Couples are allowed to have no more than $10,000 of adjusted gross income to get even a partial tax deduction for their contributions to traditional IRAs. Single or head of

If you are married and neither you nor your spouse has a retirement plan at work, your contributions to your traditional IRAs will be fully tax deductible in that year.

household filers could fully deduct their contributions to a traditional IRA if their adjusted gross income was less than $53,000. They were able to receive a partial deduction for their contributions if their adjusted gross income was between $53,000 and 63,000. Married couples filing a joint income tax return get the most bang for their bucks from Uncle Sam, who permitted them to fully deduct their IRA contributions so long as their adjusted gross income was less than $85,000. They could receive a partial deduction if their adjusted gross income was between $85,000 and 105,000. Husbands and wives are each permitted to have their own individual IRA accounts even if only one spouse is working outside the home.

To make things even more complicated (and isn't that the apparent job of government?), if one member of a married couple is an active participant in a pension plan at work, the other spouse may still deduct all of his contribution to a traditional IRA so long as the couple's combined adjusted gross income was less than $159,000 in 2008. A partial deduction for the contributions to a traditional IRA by the spouse not covered by a pension plan at work was allowed when the couple's combined adjusted gross income was between $159,000 and $169,000. At $169,000 of combined income, no deduction was permitted for a contribution to a traditional IRA for the spouse not covered by a pension at work.

Roth IRA

In a rare instance of consistency and simplicity, the contribution limits to a Roth IRA are the same as those for a traditional IRA. However, unlike a traditional IRA, which can be established by anyone with sufficient earned income, eligibility for a Roth IRA depends on your income. For example, if a single person has more than $114,000 of adjusted gross income or a married couple filing jointly has more than $169,000, they would not be eligible for a Roth IRA. No deduction of any amount is allowed for contributions to a Roth IRA. And unlike a traditional IRA, you can make contributions to a Roth IRA at any age.

TRUTH

Let's get it started
(IRA style)

Starting an IRA isn't generally something that's considered a lot of fun, so let's increase the enjoyment of the experience by giving it a little background music. Think "Let's Get It Started" as sung by the Black Eyed Peas. Hum or sing along as you think about what you need to do to take the first steps toward a secure retirement.

The first thing you need to do is to decide what kind of IRA you are going to establish. Will it be a Roth IRA or a traditional IRA? You can check your eligibility and compare the advantages of each of these IRAs elsewhere in this book.

Once you have decided what kind of IRA you are going to set up, you should decide how much money you are going to contribute to your IRA of choice. It is important to remember that although the law limits the maximum amount of money you can contribute to an IRA, it does not set a minimum amount. I certainly advise people who can afford to do so to contribute as much as law allows them to their IRAs each year. However, something is better than nothing, and it's a positive step just to get into the habit of contributing to an IRA. So if you aren't going to contribute the maximum amount permitted by law, at least commit to making some contribution to an IRA. In fact, although banks are generally not thought of as a great place to have an IRA because the investment choices are limited, they may be a good place to get your feet wet when it comes to starting an IRA.

Although the law limits the maximum amount of money you can contribute to an IRA, it does not set a minimum amount.

Most banks can set up IRAs with minimal contributions as well as minimal or even, in some cases, no fees.

But where else is a good place to start an IRA?

A mutual fund company, such as Vanguard and Fidelity, is an excellent choice as the trustee of your IRA. Mutual fund companies offer an array of investment choices, and you are sure to find a mixture of investments you'll be comfortable with. You may want to put all your IRA eggs into one basket such as a Target Mutual Fund, or you may want to spread out your IRA investment among a few different mutual funds within the same mutual fund company. The latter offers you a diverse asset allocation that can be quite helpful in planning for a safe and secure retirement.

If you want even more flexibility in picking your IRA investments, you may want to consider using the services of a brokerage firm, such as Charles Schwab, as the trustee of your IRA. With a brokerage firm, you can not only use mutual funds as the basis for your IRA investments, but you also can design your own portfolio of individual stocks and other investments for your IRA.

Fees

The same rule applies to IRAs as it does to every investment. It isn't what you make that's important; it's what you keep. Particularly with a long-term investment such as an IRA that grows either tax deferred in the case of a traditional IRA or tax free in the case of a Roth IRA, the money you lose to excessive fees is money that isn't growing and compounding for your future retirement. Fees are important. Make sure that you know all the fees involved with the particular investments and trustees that you choose.

Mutual funds have a variety of sales charges and other account maintenance charges. These are in addition to the charges you pay the trustee for managing your account. You also may have to pay an initial start-up fee when you set up your IRA and, of course, there are annual maintenance fees and fees for activities, such as sales of shares of stock that may make up your IRA's investment portfolio. Make sure that you understand all the potential fees involved with a particular trustee and a particular type of investment you're considering for your IRA.

Beneficiary designation

When you set up your IRA, you need to complete a beneficiary designation form to indicate your choice as to whom you want to receive your IRA if you die prior to having withdrawn all the money in your IRA. This is an important

> The same rule applies to IRAs as it does to every investment. It isn't what you make that's important; it's what you keep.

decision with many ramifications. You need to keep your beneficiary designation up to date because life is always changing. Deaths, births, and divorces are examples of some of the changes that may affect who you want in your beneficiary designation. A mistake in your beneficiary designation can result in your IRA passing at your death to people whom you wouldn't want to receive it or people whom you do want to receive your IRA having to pay substantially higher income taxes on the money they inherit.

Funding your IRA

It isn't necessary to fund your IRA by the end of the calendar year, although the sooner you fund it, the sooner it starts achieving tax-deferred or tax-free growth. The law permits you to make your annual contribution to your IRA as late as when your income tax return is due on April 15. Remember, however, that as generous as Uncle Sam is in allowing you to make your previous year's IRA contribution as late as three and one-half months after the end of the year that you're making the contribution for, you aren't allowed additional time to make your contribution even if you obtain an extension of the filing date for your income tax return.

TRUTH

59 1/2 and 70 1/2

Throughout the laws pertaining to withdrawals from annuities, traditional IRAs, and 401(k)s are found the recurring numbers 59 1/2 and 70 1/2. These numbers seem to take on almost mythical proportions. Most of us assume that there are logical reasons behind these numbers and assume, in particular, that the mystical 1/2 years contained in each of these numbers must have tremendous significance. However, to assume this is to give Congress much more credit than it deserves.

> The age of 59 1/2 is the age at which you can withdraw money from retirement accounts without penalties.

The age of 59 1/2 is the age at which you can withdraw money from retirement accounts without penalties. It's certainly understandable to have some kind of age prior to which there's a penalty for early withdrawal from a retirement account, because when Congress enacted the laws giving taxpayers tax breaks and inducements to save for their own retirement through these programs, allowing people to have total access at any time to these funds that are intended for retirement would just defeat the whole purpose of encouraging such savings. But why 59? And why the extra half a year to make it 59 1/2? The answer goes back to the creation of the Keogh Plan. The Keogh Plan was one of the earliest Congressional attempts to encourage people to save for their own retirement. It was named after one of its sponsors, New York Congressman Eugene Keogh. In 1962, Congress was debating the Keogh Plan's imposition of penalties before a designated "normal" retirement age and the maximum age for people to withdraw money from their tax-deferred retirement accounts so that the government could receive tax payments on the withdrawals. House and Senate committee reports indicated that the age of 60, which was a common retirement age in 1962 was, as determined by insurance company actuaries, to be actually 59 1/2 years in insurance years. No mention was made of the retirement age of 60 being 8.5714285 in dog years, but that may just be a Congressional oversight. It seemed a natural fit for Congress to conform the new retirement plan legislation with the existing policy structures then used by insurance companies, including the half-year "insurance age" designations. Thus, 59 ½ was born.

As for age 70 1/2 being the outside age at which withdrawals must be commenced from annuities, traditional IRAs, and 401(k)s to avoid tax penalties, the age of 70 has had a long history in retirement planning. In 1889, the age of 70 was used in Germany as the retirement age in the first national old-age retirement system. During the 1930s, prior to the Social Security system being enacted, about half of the state pension systems then in effect used the age of 70 as retirement age. Although for consistency's sake you might think that 70 1/2 is the insurance age equivalent to age 70, this is not correct. The 70 1/2 may have come just in an effort to make things appear consistent with the early withdrawal penalty age of 59 1/2, or it may have been chosen in response to a 1960 report of the Social Security Administration that indicated that the average life expectancy of men who would be contributing to self-employed retirement plans like the Keogh Plan was 70.45 years.

Of course, making things even more complicated are the confusing rules that indicate how the 70 1/2 mandatory withdrawal age is applied. According to the rules, you are not actually required to take out your first minimum withdrawals from your annuity, traditional IRA, or 401(k) in the year in which you turn the magic age of 70 1/2. Ironically, you are not actually required to take out your first minimum withdrawal until April 1 of the year after you turn 70 1/2. However, if you do decide to postpone your withdrawal of your first minimum withdrawal amount until that next year in an effort to further defer the payment of income taxes on the amount to be withdrawn, you put yourself in the position of having to also take out a minimum withdrawal amount for the year following the year in which you turn 70 1/2, thereby requiring you to take out two years' worth of minimum annual withdrawals in one year, which may result in a significantly larger tax hit in that year.

But what happens if you do not start taking your minimum required withdrawals in a timely fashion? Such procrastination can result in a serious penalty. Your failure to take out the minimum required distribution in a timely fashion brings with it a penalty equal to 50% of the required distribution that you did not take. The IRS has been waiting somewhat patiently to get its hands on tax money from your retirement accounts. It does not take kindly to people stretching the envelope and trying to extend the time during which they pay no taxes on their retirement accounts.

Failure to take out the minimum required distribution in a timely fashion brings with it a penalty equal to 50% of the required distribution that you did not take.

If you find that you did not take your minimum required distribution on time, you can always try to use the "dog ate my homework" defense and argue that your failure to take the proper distribution was due to a "reasonable error" on your part and that you are correcting the problem and taking the required distribution now. Doing this requires you to file an IRS Form 5329 as well as pay the 50% excess accumulation tax. Include a letter of explanation (unlike the homework example, a note from your mother will not suffice), hope for the best, and if the IRS is in a charitable mood, it may refund your excess tax penalty.

TRUTH

4

Earned income

One of the basic eligibility requirements for both a Roth and a traditional IRA is that you must have earned income in at least the amount of your contribution to the IRA, which meant that for 2008, you were able to contribute as much as $5,000 if you were younger than age 50, or $6,000 if you had reached the magic age of 50. For the years 2009 and beyond, these figures are indexed for inflation.

In determining what constitutes earned income, however, we do not use *Webster's Dictionary*, but rather that clarion of clarity, the Internal Revenue Code. In the interest of fairness, what follows is your unofficial decoder.

First the easy part. According to the IRS, wages you earn at work qualify as earned income. In fact, the IRS doesn't just consider your wages, but also any tips, commissions, or bonuses you receive. An easy way to determine whether your income qualifies as earned income is to look at your Form W-2. Any compensation indicated in box 1 of your W-2 generally qualifies as earned income.

Earned income does not include compensation or income you receive as a result of earnings and profits from rental income property. It also does not include income derived as interest, dividend income, or capital gains.

Earned income for IRA purposes also specifically does not include any income you receive from a pension, annuity, or deferred compensation. Neither does it include amounts that you do not declare as income on your income tax return, such as disability payments or Social Security payments.

> One of the basic eligibility requirements for both a Roth and a traditional IRA is that you must have earned income in at least the amount of your contribution to the IRA.

More exotically, any income that is excluded from your gross income for income tax purposes through the Foreign Earned Income rules is not considered earned income for IRA eligibility purposes.

If you are self-employed either as a sole proprietor of a business or even a partner, your earned income is defined as the net earnings from your business reduced by the amount of any contributions made on your behalf to any retirement plan and minus the deduction allowed for half of your self-employment taxes. If you are particularly industrious and are a salaried employee who also has a business on the side, you can take the total of your taxable compensation from your wages and your own business to determine the total amount of your earned income for purposes of IRA eligibility. Hopefully, you are making more than $5,000 per year from your job and your own business so that you will be eligible for the full contribution amount to an IRA.

However, income that you receive from a partnership that is primarily an investment and not a partnership in which you actually provide substantial services is not considered earned income for purposes of eligibility to contribute to an IRA. For instance, income derived from investment in limited partnerships holding real estate in which your only participation in the enterprise is investing your money as a limited partner and receiving distributions from the partnership as determined by the general partner are not considered earned income for IRA eligibility purposes.

Loophole 1

If your business expenses end up eliminating the profit of your self-employment income, you are still able to take as your earned income, for purposes of IRA eligibility, the gross amount earned through your self-employment.

For divorced people, just as alimony received is considered to be taxable income for income tax purposes, so is alimony received considered to be earned income for purposes of determining your eligibility to contribute to an IRA. In fact, some divorced people consider their alimony as perhaps the most dearly earned income they get. However, just as child support is not considered taxable income, neither is child support considered earned income for purposes of IRA eligibility.

For those of you remaining married and filing a joint income tax return, even if one spouse does not receive earned income, both spouses can have their own IRAs so long as there is sufficient income to qualify for two IRAs. In 2008, a couple had to have an income of at least $10,000 unless both of them were over the age of 50, in which case they needed to have at least $12,000 of earned income to qualify for maximum contributions to separate IRAs for each of them.

Loophole 2

There is no minimum age requirement for establishing and contributing to an IRA. So if your child or grandchild has earned income, she can establish her own IRA and start herself on the road to tax-deferred or tax-free compounding of her funds depending on whether she chooses a traditional or a Roth IRA. Particularly for a young child with earned income, the Roth IRA is the better choice. It is possible that a child can have enough earned money to qualify for the maximum contribution to an IRA ($5,000 in 2008) and not have enough other income to require her to pay either Social Security taxes or income taxes on her earned income. Paying a child for work actually performed in a parent's business or even for performing household chores can result in earned income that can set the child on the road to a sizeable IRA later in life. With the magic of compound tax-free interest over a long period, even if the contributions to a Roth IRA for the child only occurred between the ages of 7 and 18 years, the child would have millions by the age of 65.

Many of the major brokerage firms and mutual fund families are willing to open a custodial IRA for a minor so long as a parent or guardian cosigns the documents as the child's guardian. Some brokerage houses offer custodial IRAs for children with no minimum balance requirements and no annual maintenance fees. Others require a small minimum balance or a small annual maintenance fee. As always, however, I caution you to precisely follow all the rules and laws in regard to properly reporting the payments for such services and the establishment of a child's IRA.

TRUTH

IRA deductions

One of the primary attractions of a traditional IRA is the ability to deduct your contributions. This enables you to pay no income tax on the money you earned and contributed to your traditional IRA at the time that you contributed to your traditional IRA. Instead, income taxes are deferred until you withdraw the money from your traditional IRA, most likely years later in retirement.

However, one of the unfortunate misconceptions about deducting contributions to a traditional IRA is that you may deduct the entire amount of your contribution in all circumstances. Unfortunately, this is not true. If neither you nor your spouse actively participated in an employer-sponsored retirement plan, you are eligible to deduct the full amount of your contributions to IRAs for both of you. But if either of you were an active participant in an employer-sponsored retirement plan, the amount of your tax deduction for your traditional IRA contributions is limited. For example, if you contributed to a 401(k) plan at work, you would not be able to deduct the full amount of your contribution to a traditional IRA

Fortunately, determining whether you were covered by an employer-sponsored retirement plan is quite simple. Merely look at your W-2, and you will see a box designated as "Retirement Plan." If it is checked, you were covered by the employer's plan. Even if you have a 401(k) plan available to you at work, you are not considered an active participant and consequently disqualified from making fully deductible contributions to a traditional IRA unless you actually participate in the plan.

If either you or your spouse were an active participant in an employer-sponsored retirement plan during any part of the year, the

> One of the unfortunate misconceptions about deducting contributions to a traditional IRA is that you may deduct the entire amount of your contribution in all circumstances. Unfortunately, this is not true.

amount of your deductible contribution to a traditional IRA may be reduced or even eliminated depending on your income as well as your tax-filing status.

The definition of your income used to determine traditional IRA contribution deductibility is your Modified Adjusted Gross Income (MAGI). This is calculated by determining your Adjusted Gross Income (AGI) and then adding certain other income to it to determine your MAGI. Your AGI is the amount of your total income including wages, interest, retirement account income, capital gains, and alimony minus certain specific adjustments to your income, such as deductible IRA contributions, 401(k) contributions, alimony payments, and interest on student loans. It is shown on line 38 of Form 1040. Once you have determined your AGI, to determine your MAGI, you add back other specific sources of income, such as deductions claimed for student loan interest, to arrive at your MAGI. Most people's MAGI is the same as their AGI.

In 2008, if you were covered by a retirement plan at work and you filed your income tax return as either single or as head of household, you were entitled to deduct the full amount of your traditional IRA contribution if you had no more than $53,000 of MAGI. If your income was more than $53,000 but less than $63,000, you were entitled to a partial deduction. The amount of your deduction may be calculated on forms found in IRS Publication 590. If your income is $63,000 or more, you may not deduct any of your contribution to your traditional IRA. Even if you are not eligible to deduct any of your contribution to your traditional IRA, an IRA is still a good investment in your retirement; however, if you are eligible for a Roth IRA, you are better off making a Roth IRA your IRA of choice for your nondeductible contribution.

In 2008, if you were covered by a retirement plan at work and you filed your income tax return jointly with your spouse, you were entitled to deduct the full amount of your traditional IRA contribution if you had no more than $85,000 of MAGI. If your income was more than $85,000 but less than $105,000, you were entitled to a partial deduction that, again, may be calculated on forms found in IRS Publication 590.

In 2008, for those of you filing in the IRS's least favorite status, as "married filing separately," you were only entitled to deduct the full amount of your traditional IRA contribution if you had less than $10,000 of MAGI. If you had $10,000 or more of MAGI, you were prohibited from taking any deduction for your contribution to a traditional IRA. Obviously, however, if your MAGI is as low as $10,000, it is unlikely that you will be thinking much about funding an IRA.

Loophole

If you are married but filing separately, as when you are in the midst of a divorce and you are not living with your spouse, the IRS permits you to be considered "single" for purposes of determining IRA deductibility eligibility.

In 2008, if you were not covered by a retirement plan at work and you filed your income taxes as single, head of household, or married filing either jointly or separately with a spouse who is also not an active participant in an employer retirement plan, you could deduct the full amount of your traditional IRA contribution.

In 2008, if you were married filing jointly with a spouse who is an active participant in an employer retirement plan, you were still entitled to fully deduct your traditional IRA contribution if your MAGI was no more than $156,000 if you were not covered by a retirement plan at work. If your income was more than $159,000 but less than $169,000, you were entitled to a partial deduction. Once your MAGI reached $169,000, you lost your eligibility to have any of your traditional IRA contribution tax deductible.

And, of course, for the lepers of the income tax filing world, those married filing separately, if you are not covered by a plan at work but your spouse is, you are eligible for only a partial deduction of your traditional IRA contribution, and only when your MAGI is less than $10,000. Fortunately, however, you can be considered "single" for IRA contribution deduction purposes if you do not live with your spouse during the year.

TRUTH

6

Distributions from IRAs

According to the great Supreme Court Justice Oliver Wendell Holmes, "No generalization is worth a damn, including this one." Holmes was not talking about distributions from IRAs, but he could have been.

There are a number of generalizations about distributions from IRAs that are either confusing or downright wrong. Here are a couple of them.

Generalization 1: All distributions from traditional IRAs are taxable

Whether you are taxed on the distributions you take from your traditional IRA depends on whether you deducted your contributions to the traditional IRA. Although many people are able to deduct the full amount of the contributions they make to their traditional IRAs over the years, some people are not able to deduct any of their contributions to a traditional IRA, while others are only able to deduct a portion of their annual contributions to their IRAs. The key to the deductibility of your contributions to your traditional IRA depends on your tax filing status (single, head of household, married filing jointly, or married filing separately), whether you are covered by a retirement plan at work, and the amount of your adjusted gross income as determined on your income tax return.

For example, if a man and his wife, filing a joint income tax return, are not covered by a retirement plan at work, they both can deduct the full amount of their allowed annual contribution to their respective IRAs. However, if a man filing a joint income tax return with his wife is covered by a retirement plan at work, in 2008 he was able to deduct only the full amount of his contribution to an IRA if he and his wife's adjusted gross income was less than $85,000. If their adjusted gross income was between $85,000 and $105,000, the man could deduct a portion of his deduction as determined by filling in the worksheet found in IRS

> There are a number of generalizations about distributions from IRAs that are either confusing or downright wrong.

Publication 590. If the couple's adjusted gross income was $105,000 or more, the man could not make a tax-deductible contribution to his traditional IRA in that year.

Your eligibility to make a tax-deductible contribution to a traditional IRA is made anew each year. Just because you are ineligible to make a tax deductible contribution in one year in no way negates your ability to make a tax-deductible contribution in subsequent years if your income meets the deductibility standards. Even if you are unable to make a fully tax-deductible contribution to your traditional IRA, it still makes sense to invest the maximum amount of your permissible contribution to your traditional IRA and take the deduction on the portion that is allowed by law. However, if it's apparent that your income is going to be consistently higher than what will allow you to make tax-deductible contributions to a traditional IRA, you should consider converting your traditional IRA to a Roth IRA, if you qualify, and have your nondeductible contributions grow tax free and without minimum distribution requirements in the future. You need to pay income taxes on the deductible portion of your traditional IRA that you convert, but you can spread out the conversion of your traditional IRA over a period of years, if necessary, to reduce the immediate tax effects of converting. Ultimately, you will be better off.

> If you make nondeductible contributions to your traditional IRA, the amount of those nondeductible contributions are not subject to income tax when you take a distribution from your IRA.

When you take distributions from your traditional IRA, if all your contributions to your IRA are tax deductible, all the distributions you take are taxable. However, if you make nondeductible contributions to your traditional IRA, the amount of those nondeductible contributions are not subject to income tax when you take a distribution from your IRA. If you do take distributions from a traditional IRA into which you have made nondeductible as well as deductible contributions, a portion of your distribution is considered to be a return of your nondeductible contributions, a portion is attributed to your nondeductible contributions, and the remaining portion is the gain from your investments' growth (hopefully). Until all your nondeductible contributions have been distributed to you, each distribution you take is only partially taxable. Although this may seem complicated, it is easy to determine through the use of worksheets provided in IRS Publication 590 and IRS Form 8606. If you make nondeductible contributions to a traditional IRA, keep your computations and Form 8606 for each year that you make those nondeductible contributions to make it easier to determine the taxability of your required withdrawals when you start to take them.

Generalization 2: You must pay income taxes on all amounts you take out of your Roth IRA within the first five years

This is a common misconception. The truth is that the five-year rule only applies to the "earnings" of your Roth IRA. You've already paid income taxes on the money you've used to fund your Roth IRA, so it stands to reason that you won't be subject to income tax when you take that money out of your Roth IRA. This is so reasonable a position that even the IRS, which is thought by some to be notoriously unreasonable, accepts this reasoning and never subjects to income tax any of the money that you take out of your Roth IRA up to the amount of your contributions. The five-year rule applies only to the earnings of your Roth IRA. You may not take out those earnings from your Roth IRA without subjecting them to tax unless you are at least 59 1/2 years old and have had the Roth IRA in effect for at least five years. But even here, there are exceptions, such as when you need the money because you are disabled.

TRUTH

7

Minimum required distributions

According to the 15th century English proverb, "All good things must come to an end." Although tax deferral of the compounding value of traditional IRAs and traditional 401(k)s did not exist in 15th century England, this particular old English proverb certainly applies to both of these retirement savings vehicles.

Tax laws are written not merely to take your money but to also encourage certain activities and discourage other activities. Anything that permits you to put off paying income taxes is certain to be popular. So when the federal government wants to encourage us to save for our own retirement, making traditional IRAs and traditional 401(k)s tax deferred adds considerably to their popularity and use.

One possible advantage to deferring taxes is an assumption that many people have that when they defer paying taxes on money that has been compounding on a tax-deferred basis in a traditional IRA or a traditional 401(k) until the time of our retirement, they will be in a lower income tax bracket so that not only did they put off paying income taxes, but also when they eventually do pay income taxes on the money saved in these retirement accounts, they will be paying at a lower rate. Fortunately, even if this assumption is incorrect due either to the income tax laws changing or their having more taxable income in their retirement than anticipated, the benefit of having retirement investments compound on a tax-deferred basis is still a tremendous advantage that allows more retirement dollars to work over time undiminished by taxes until retirement.

In keeping with what must be an unwritten IRS policy, the rules for the minimum amount that you must take out of your traditional IRA or traditional 401(k) are somewhat confusing.

But eventually Uncle Sam wants his money. When it comes to traditional IRAs and traditional 401(k)s, eventually means that you must, at age 70 1/2 if you have not already done so, start to take money out of your traditional IRA or traditional 401(k) and pay income taxes on the money that you withdraw. In keeping with what must be an unwritten IRS policy, the rules for the minimum amount that you must take out of your traditional IRA or traditional 401(k) are somewhat confusing. You are not actually required to take out money from either of these retirement accounts in the year that you turn 70 1/2, but rather, you can legally postpone taking your first minimum required distribution from your traditional IRA or traditional 401(k) until April Fools Day of the year after the year you turn 70 1/2. As Will Rogers said, "I don't know jokes. I just watch Congress and report the facts."

But the joke continues.

The first distribution that you are required to take for the year in which you turn 70 1/2 may be taken in the next calendar year, but the distribution for the second year must be taken by December 31 in that year as well. This means that if you put off taking your first distribution until the year after you turn 70 1/2, you will end up having to take two distributions in one year. Obviously, this could have a potentially serious affect on your income tax bill by putting you into a higher tax bracket. In addition, increasing your income in that manner could lead to as much as 85% of your Social Security benefits being subject to income tax.

As complicated as determining when to start taking your required minimum distributions is, calculating how much you need to take from your traditional IRA or traditional 401(k) is surprisingly easy. In 2002, the IRS simplified the method for calculating minimum required distributions. Some people think the IRS did this less to make things easier for taxpayers than because it believed the complexity of the former system might have contributed to confused, but well-meaning, taxpayers paying less in taxes. But whatever the reason for the changes, the result is that they are more favorable to taxpayers than previously.

You start your calculations by taking the balance of your traditional IRA or traditional 401(k) as of December 31 of the previous year. Then you divide that number by the figure corresponding to your age in the IRS' Uniform Lifetime Table. (You can download a PDF of this table, named AppC_Table, from the book's Web site at www.ftpress. com/store/product.aspx?isbn=0132333848.) For example, if your traditional IRA or traditional 401(k) contains $100,000 and you are

71 years old, the divisor figure from the Uniform Lifetime Table is 26.5 which, when applied to your traditional IRA or traditional 401(k) balance, would result in a minimum required distribution amount of $3,773.58 for that year. Each year, you repeat the process by applying the divisor figure that corresponds to your age in that particular year. The Uniform Lifetime Table goes all the way up to 115. For those people reaching the age of 116 or older, the IRS gives its version of a Senior Citizen Discount and merely applies the divisor figure for someone 115 years old, which is 1.9.

However, if your spouse is more than ten years younger than you and she is the sole beneficiary of your traditional IRA or traditional 401(k), you may use the Joint Life Expectancy Table or, as I refer to it, the Derek Table, named after Hollywood actor and director John Derek who married, in order, three gorgeous look-alike actresses: Ursula Andress, Linda Evans, and finally Bo Derek, all of whom were at least ten years younger than he was at the time of their marriages. For example, if the 71-year-old person from the example in the previous paragraph was married to a 50-year-old woman, he would have a divisor of 35 according to the Derek Table, so his minimum required distribution would be $2,857.14.

Of course, these calculations are only for minimum required withdrawals. There is nothing preventing you from taking out more than your minimum required distribution amount in any year that you choose. The only drawback is that whatever amount you withdraw from your traditional IRA or traditional 401(k) is subject to income taxes in the year that you take out the money. And in any particular year, you cannot use the money that you take out in excess of your minimum required distribution amount to reduce the amount that you are required to take in the next year.

In keeping with what must be an unwritten IRS policy, the rules for the minimum amount that you must take out of your traditional IRA or traditional 401(k) are somewhat confusing.

TRUTH

Withdrawal pains

Putting money into a traditional IRA is not a particularly difficult task. Uncle Sam, in fact, encourages you to save for your retirement by providing, in some circumstances, a tax deduction and tax deferral on the income earned by money invested in a traditional IRA. But when it comes to taking that money out before the magic age of 59 1/2, your rich uncle is much less cooperative. Withdrawals from a traditional IRA before you reach the age of 59 1/2 not only results in your having to pay income tax at ordinary income tax rates on the funds you withdraw, but in addition, you will be hit with a 10% excise tax as well.

Fortunately, there are loopholes.

Taking substantially equal yearly payments made over your life expectancy as determined by IRS charts provides an exception to the premature withdrawal penalties. However, as good as this exception may appear, it is actually even better because your yearly payments do not actually have to be taken throughout your entire IRS determined life expectancy, but only until you have reached the age of 59 1/2 years or for five years, whichever comes first. It isn't logical; it's the IRS. Don't even look for logic.

Further indication that Uncle Sam has a heart are the rules that permit you to take early withdrawals from your traditional IRA penalty free for college or other "qualified higher education expenses." These expenses can include tuition, fees, books, supplies, and equipment such as computers for yourself, your spouse, your children, or your grandchildren.

Rules that permit you to take early withdrawals from your traditional IRA penalty free for college or other "qualified higher education expenses."

Another exception to the early withdrawal rules involves the payment of medical expenses. If you become permanently disabled or need to use the money to pay for prolonged medical treatment as a result of a serious illness or injury, you can take the money out of your IRA without penalty so long as the medical costs meet the conditions for deductibility of medical costs of being more than 7.5%

of your adjusted gross income. Another medically related exception to the early withdrawal rules is that if you need to use money from your traditional IRA to pay for the premiums for health insurance, you can do so without being penalized by the IRS for an early withdrawal so long as you have been on unemployment for more than 12 weeks.

Probably the most interesting and confusing exception is the IRS rule for taking an early withdrawal as a first-time homebuyer.

However, probably the most interesting and confusing exception is the IRS rule for taking an early withdrawal as a first-time homebuyer. According to IRS rules, you are permitted to take as much as $10,000 as an early distribution from your traditional IRA without a penalty if you are under the age of 59 1/2 and you use the money to buy a first home. As always, there are additional requirements you must meet to avail yourself of this helpful loophole.

First, the home that you are buying must be for your use as a principal residence. Additionally, you can qualify for this exception even if you use the money from your traditional IRA to pay for a first-time home purchase by your spouse, child, grandchild, parent, or grandparent.

Next comes the condition that makes my head spin like the little girl in the movie *The Exorcist.* To qualify as a first-time homebuyer, you must not have owned a home during the preceding two years. In other words, if you owned a home six years ago, sold it two years later, and bought another home that you then sold two years after that and now two years later are seeking to buy another home, you still qualify under this rule as a first-time homebuyer. To an IRS agent this is logical. Not one to look a gift horse or IRS agent in the mouth, I will continue to be confused by the terminology "first-time homebuyer," but I thank Uncle Sam that I can potentially utilize the first-time home buyer exception multiple times.

The IRS has further conditions on the use of the first-time homebuyer exception to the early withdrawal penalty, but none of them are particularly onerous or difficult to meet. You must use the money that you take out of your traditional IRA for the cost of buying, building, or rebuilding a home, although you can also use the funds to help pay for the costs of financing and settlement costs. You also must use the money within 120 days of when you withdraw it from your traditional IRA, so it is best to make sure that the actual purchase of the home is going to occur in a timely fashion before you withdraw the money, although there would be no reason to take the money out any earlier than you would need to because, by waiting as long as possible, you can continue your income tax deferral a bit longer. Again, using tortured IRS logic, the IRS determines the purchase date to be the date when you sign the Purchase and Sales Agreement to buy the home rather than the actual date that the deed to the property is transferred to you. If the sale does not go through after the signing of the contract, you must put the money back into the traditional IRA within 120 days to avoid income tax and penalties. The best policy is to wait until you are ready to actually receive title to the property to take the money from your IRA.

All good things must come to an end. The first-time homebuyer exception to the early withdrawal penalties is not without limit. Although you can qualify any number of times for a first-time homebuyer exception, the IRS limits the total amount of money that you can withdraw penalty free from your traditional IRA for this purpose to no more than $10,000 over your lifetime.

TRUTH

9

Spousal IRA

Marriage has many benefits, most of which are outside of the purview of this book, but one that definitely is not is the Spousal IRA. Generally, among the requirements for people setting up an IRA to take advantage of the tax-deferred or tax-free benefits provided by a traditional IRA or a Roth IRA is that the person setting up the IRA has earned income from wages, commissions, or self-employment. However, there is one major exception to this rule. Married couples may set up and contribute to two separate IRAs even though only one is employed. A Spousal IRA does not have to be a new IRA. In fact, it is common for the Spousal IRA rules to be applied when a spouse opened her own IRA while she was working, may no longer be employed (perhaps she's now a stay-at-home parent), and now will be receiving contributions to her IRA from her spouse under the Spousal IRA rules. Although the other spouse may supply the funds for a Spousal IRA, the IRA belongs to the spouse for whom the IRA is set up. There are no joint IRAs.

In 2008, a nonemployed spouse was eligible for a contribution to a traditional IRA of as much as $5,000 (or $6,000 if she were 50 or older) so long as the couple filed a joint income tax return and the employed spouse had enough earned income to cover the amount of the contribution. Obviously, requiring the working spouse to earn $10,000 (or $12,000 if both are over 50) is not a difficult condition to meet. The actual money used to fund the nonemployed spouse's traditional IRA can come from anywhere, even a gift from relatives, if the working spouse earned enough to support the contribution. So far this is pretty simple.

> Married couples may set up and contribute to two separate IRAs even though only one is employed.

Now it gets complicated.

To qualify for a fully deductible contribution to a traditional spousal IRA, where the working spouse is covered by a qualified retirement plan at work, the couple's joint adjusted gross income as shown on their joint income tax return must be less than $159,000. A partial deduction for the nonworking spouse's traditional Spousal IRA is permitted when the couple's adjusted gross income is between $159,000 and $169,000. As always, to determine the amount of a partial deduction, you should go to IRS Publication 590 for the precise steps to calculate the amount of your deduction. As for the working spouse's ability to make a deductible contribution to his own traditional IRA, it is phased out between $85,000 and $105,000 of adjusted gross income. However, if neither spouse is covered by a qualified retirement plan, there are no income limitations on the

> Because contributions to a Roth IRA are, in all circumstances, made with nondeductible, after-tax contributions, the whole issue of deductibility is a nonissue.

deductibility of the contributions of either spouse to his or her traditional IRA.

If both spouses are employed and participating in qualified retirement plans, their joint adjusted gross income must be less than $85,000 to make contributions to their respective traditional IRAs fully deductible. Once again, they may be able to take partial deductions when their joint income is between $85,000 and $105,000.

Then comes the Roth.

Because contributions to a Roth IRA are, in all circumstances, made with nondeductible, after-tax contributions, the whole issue of deductibility is a nonissue. However, you still must qualify to have a Roth IRA in the first place. The law phases out the ability to contribute to a Roth IRA for couples with adjusted gross incomes between $159,000 and $169,000 for married couples filing joint income tax returns. As an indication of Uncle Sam's low opinion of people who are married but file separate returns, the eligibility for contributing to a Roth IRA begins to phase out at dollar one of adjusted gross income and is totally phased out at only $10,000, which effectively takes away Spousal Roth IRAs as an option.

More rules

If your spouse is opening or contributing to a traditional Spousal IRA, he must be under the age of 70 1/2. In contrast, there are no such age restrictions for a person opening a Roth IRA. When the Spousal IRA is opened, regardless of where the money came from to fund it, it must be titled in the name of the spouse it is being set up for. Her Social Security number should be used in regard to the Spousal IRA even if the money came from her husband's earnings.

TIP If traditional IRAs are being used and, between the two spouses, they are not making the maximum contribution to both IRAs, they may be better off making the lion's share of their IRA contributions to the IRA of the younger of the spouses to delay mandatory distributions and prolong tax deferral.

TRUTH

Trusts as IRA beneficiaries

It is most common for people to name individual people as the beneficiaries of their IRAs, but there can be many reasons for naming a trust as the beneficiary. Some of these reasons include

- Minors will be inheriting your IRA. Without a trust, their guardian will manage the inherited IRA on behalf of the minor until the minor reaches the age of 18, but at that age, total control of the entire IRA must be turned over to the young but no longer minor child.

- Your beneficiaries may not be minors, but they have already shown a lack of ability to properly manage money and make wise financial decisions.

- Your beneficiaries may be disabled or have special needs. Through the use of a properly established trust, you not only can provide for management of the IRA's funds on their behalf, but also you can create the trust in a way that would allow the money in the IRA to be used to supplement any state or federal benefits to which they might otherwise be entitled without affecting their eligibility for such governmental programs.

- You may want to provide for a spouse of a second or subsequent marriage while preserving assets for children from an earlier marriage. This can be done through a type of trust called a Qualified Terminable Interest Property trust, or QTIP.

Although, for the previous reasons or others, a trust may be a desirable choice as the beneficiary of an IRA, naming a trust as an IRA beneficiary is a complicated matter. One of the initial concerns is that trusts are subject to income tax at a significantly higher rate than individuals. The simplest way to avoid this problem is to use a Roth IRA to fund the trust, because the income that the trust earned would be income tax free. If your estate and financial planning includes a trust as an IRA beneficiary, you may want to consider converting any traditional IRAs you may have to Roth IRAs.

Naming a trust as an IRA beneficiary is a complicated matter.

A picky little detail

If, for instance, Homer Simpson were to choose to leave his IRA to his three minor children Lisa, Bart, and Maggie, he could do so in trust (particularly because of concern for Bart's financial management abilities). However, the tremendous tax deferral or, in the case of a Roth IRA, tax avoidance benefits of a Stretch IRA for the three children would be somewhat mitigated by the legal requirement that, when a trust is the beneficiary of an IRA, the life expectancy used to measure the Stretch period of distributions is based on the life expectancy of the oldest of the beneficiaries, or in this case Lisa. In this example, Maggie, the youngest beneficiary, might be losing out on many years of further tax-deferred or tax-free growth. However, Homer could avoid this problem by making three separate trusts, one for each of the children, as the designated equal beneficiaries of the IRA.

To take advantage of the rules that permit a Stretch IRA, a trust beneficiary of an IRA must meet the following conditions:

- The trust must be valid under applicable state law.

- The individual beneficiaries must be identifiable from the trust document.

- The trust either must be irrevocable at the time that it is created, or as occurs more often, become irrevocable when the initial IRA owner dies.

- Copies of the trust must be supplied to the administrator of the IRA in a timely basis.

- The actual beneficiaries of the trust must be individual people.

These conditions are not particularly difficult to meet. A competent estate-planning lawyer can easily prepare a trust that is valid under the laws of the state where the IRA owner lives. As for identifying the beneficiaries of the trust, generally you want to name specific people, such as your children, as the beneficiaries of your trust. Even if you provide for a deceased child's share to pass to his own children or if he has no children to pass to his siblings, these people are readily identifiable. Because the trust, to qualify as a proper IRA beneficiary, does not have to be irrevocable until the death of the original IRA owner, it is common and gives the IRA owner the greatest amount of flexibility to have the trust be fully amendable by him until death, at which point the trust becomes automatically irrevocable. In this way, the IRA owner can adapt and change the trust in any way to meet changing family needs right up until his death. Although providing a copy of the trust is not required until the IRA owner dies, there is no reason not to provide the IRA administrator with a copy of the trust as well as any amendments to the trust that are made during the IRA owner's lifetime. The requirement that actual beneficiaries of the trust must be individual people is easy to comply with because it merely means that you must designate the people who will receive payments from the trust.

There are other complicated rules that deal with various aspects of naming a trust as a beneficiary of an IRA, but they, too, do not represent conditions that are particularly difficult to comply with. In fact, in a complicated situation when the IRA owner may wish to provide for the use of disclaimers and division of benefits and take the benefit of Stretch IRA provisions, it may be simpler to use a trust to set out the desired hierarchy of beneficiaries than to do it on a standard beneficiary designation form, particularly when some plan administrators may balk at complicated beneficiary designations.

TRUTH

11

Beneficiary designations

Every owner of an IRA or a 401(k) should have an up-to-date beneficiary designation form that indicates who will receive the funds remaining in the IRA or 401(k) upon his death. If there is no beneficiary designation form or if the form is lost, the money is passed to the estate of the IRA or 401(k) owner, with adverse income tax consequences.

Warning

Many people fail to keep their beneficiary designations current. You should review these forms regularly, particularly as family circumstances change as a result of births, marriages, deaths, or divorces. You can change your beneficiary designations whenever you choose. However, if you neglect to remove a former spouse from your beneficiary statement, your ex-spouse could receive that money regardless of your divorce. If you do not list anyone as your beneficiary or if the people you list predecease you, the money goes to your estate. That means the money has to come out over the next five years rather than having the payments stretched out over the lifetimes of children or grandchildren whom you might have wanted to name as your beneficiaries. In addition, having your estate as the beneficiary brings the entire IRA or 401(k) into the probate process, which can increase the costs and time to transfer the account.

> If you neglect to remove a former spouse from your beneficiary statement, your ex-spouse could receive that money regardless of your divorce.

Loophole

Looking at the glass as half full rather than half empty (and dirty to boot), if you find yourself in the unfortunate position of having to take out inherited IRA money over a five-year period, you should remember that IRS rules do not require you to take out the IRA money equally over the five-year period. The only requirement is that all the money comes out of the IRA by December 31 of the fifth year following the death of the IRA account owner. Therefore, if you inherit an IRA through an estate, you at least have the opportunity to leave the money in the IRA for more than five years to gain even more compound interest during that time. As always, however, there are complicated exceptions to the rules. If the deceased person whose IRA is being inherited was at least 70 1/2 at the time of his death, minimum distributions must be made to the estate by the IRA in accordance with the remaining life expectancy as calculated for the year of the death of the deceased IRA owner.

It is an unfortunate fact that banks and other financial institutions that act as IRA or 401(k) custodians and administrators sometimes lose beneficiary designation forms. This is a particular problem when banks get taken over by other banks. The best protection from lost beneficiary forms is for you to keep a duplicate copy of the beneficiary designation form that the IRA or 401(k) custodian or administrator has acknowledged.

The forms that the custodians or administrators supply often do not leave enough room for you to indicate who will be the primary beneficiary and contingent beneficiaries. If this happens to you, you can adapt the form supplied by the custodian or administrator to provide for all the beneficiaries you may wish to list. If you are naming children as beneficiaries, it is particularly important to also list who will get a deceased child's share. In the case of children or grandchildren, you may also want to name one or more trusts as a beneficiary. Doing so can enable the tax savings on an IRA or 401(k) to be stretched out for as much as 70 years or more.

The most common choice of a beneficiary of an IRA or a 401(k) for a married person is that person's spouse. A surviving spouse is allowed to merely roll the inherited IRA into his own IRA without tax consequences, which can provide additional planning opportunities. Also, if your spouse is more than ten years younger than you are, naming your spouse as your primary beneficiary permits you to reduce the amount of the required distributions you must take from your 401(k) or traditional IRA at age 70 1/2. This doesn't mean that

> The most common choice of a beneficiary of an IRA or a 401(k) for a married person is that person's spouse.

you're limited in the amount that you may take, but it does permit you to increase the value of the tax-deferral in your traditional IRA or 401(k) account by taking only your minimum required distributions.

Another sensible choice is to name children as contingent secondary beneficiaries. In this way, not only might the children inherit the IRA or 401(k) upon the death of the IRA or 401(k) account owner, but also if the surviving spouse did not need some or all of the inherited account, some or all of the inherited IRA could be disclaimed and passed directly to the children, who would then be in a position to defer or, in the case of a Roth IRA or Roth 401(k), avoid paying income taxes on the funds in the account as they took required payments based on their projected life expectancy as determined by IRS charts. Providing additional flexibility is the fact that the law gives you up to nine months after the date of the death of the retirement account holder to decide whether to disclaim an interest in the retirement account.

> **A 15-year-old who inherits a traditional IRA can spread out taking the payments over a life expectancy of 67 years and achieve a significant tax deferral.**

You can achieve even more tax deferral by having a trust for grandchildren as a beneficiary. In this way, you can spread out the distributions over the lives of the grandchildren. For example, a 15-year-old who inherits a traditional IRA can spread out taking the payments over a life expectancy of 67 years and achieve a significant tax deferral. If the same 15-year-old child inherited a Roth IRA, she would be required to take out the funds over her life expectancy but would not be liable for income taxes on the money received.

TRUTH

12

Customizing beneficiary designation forms

The beneficiary designation form on your IRA or 401(k) represents one of the most important documents you will ever have. It is the form where you list who is to get the benefits of your retirement account after your death. All the tremendous benefits for future tax-deferred or tax-free compound growth can be drastically reduced or even lost if you don't fill in the form properly or keep it up to date.

The forms, as provided by the administrator of your retirement account, are pretty basic, simple forms, and therein lies part of the problem. Although the funds in your retirement account may be hundreds of thousands of dollars and represent an asset that requires somewhat complicated planning to best effectuate your wishes both as to who shall receive these funds upon your death and under what circumstances they shall receive these benefits, the forms may be a bit cramped to include all the necessary terms and information necessary to customize the form to your particular situation. In addition, to take advantage of the benefits of the Stretch IRA and a properly executed Disclaimer through which tremendous flexibility and tax savings can be achieved, you may need more space than is provided in the beneficiary designation form that your plan administrator provides.

> The forms, as provided by the administrator of your retirement account, are pretty basic, simple forms, and therein lies part of the problem.

Danger

If you don't keep your beneficiary designation current and it leaves your retirement account to people no longer living, at your death the assets in your 401(k) or IRA may pass by default to your estate, with the beneficiaries to be determined in accordance with your will or, if you have no will, according to your state's laws of intestacy, which state the order of who inherits your assets if you do not have a will. The good thing is that the same people whom you would want to get the benefit of your 401(k) or IRA may still inherit these assets through your will or the laws of intestacy. However, the bad thing is that if they inherit your retirement assets through your estate, they generally are not in a position to take advantage of the tremendous benefits of a Stretch IRA.

The key to an effective beneficiary designation is recognizing that it is a living document. Once you have determined who will be your beneficiaries, you cannot just put the form away and forget about it. Life is all about change. Births, deaths, marriages, and perhaps most of all divorces can have a serious effect on who you want (or don't want) to inherit your 401(k) or IRA. Failing to vigilantly keep your beneficiary designation up to date can result in people you want to inherit your assets not being able to do so or, even worse, someone like an ex-spouse inheriting your assets.

TIP Review your beneficiary designation when there is a major change in the laws that might affect your beneficiary decisions. You should also review your beneficiary designation when there is a major change in your family circumstances, such as a birth, death, marriage or divorce. If you do change your beneficiary designation, make sure that you have your new beneficiary designation form signed off on and acknowledged as being accepted by your 401(k) or IRA custodian, and keep a copy of the signed document. Forms get lost. If the custodian of your 401(k) or IRA misplaces or loses your form, if you do not have an authenticated copy of the form, you can be subject to the default position of your plan, which may not be what you want.

Things to consider when customizing your beneficiary designation form

- Do you want the beneficiaries of your 401(k) or IRA to inherit it by right of representation such that, for instance, if you have a child who predeceases you, that deceased child's children would inherit his share of the 401(k) or IRA?

- Do you want a trust to hold the funds for a minor or someone else who you think would benefit by having the funds managed and controlled on that person's behalf? The rules for having a trust as a 401(k) or IRA beneficiary are somewhat complicated and described in Truth 10.

- If you are married, have you provided for where the 401(k) or IRA will pass if you and your spouse die simultaneously?

Most plan administrators are somewhat accommodating when it comes to permitting customized beneficiary designation forms, but only if the provisions contained in the customized beneficiary designation form do not conflict with the terms and conditions of the particular plan. If you find that your IRA custodian does not cooperate with what you want to do to customize your beneficiary designation form, you can transfer your IRA to another custodian who will be more accommodating.

Most plan administrators are somewhat accommodating when it comes to permitting customized beneficiary designation forms.

Finally, make sure that the executor of your estate is aware of who is designated as the beneficiaries of your 401(k) or IRA. This information is important not just for proper estate tax and income tax purposes, but also to make sure that your wishes as to your retirement account are fulfilled.

TRUTH

Self-directed IRAs

Boring is not necessarily a bad thing when it comes to investing. Some of the most profitable investing over time is done through index mutual funds, which provide steady growth and low fees. Many people invest in the usual stocks, bonds, and mutual funds in their IRAs, and there is nothing wrong with that. However, IRA investments are in no way limited to these conventional investments. Subject, of course, to some rules and limitations of the IRS, there is a world of intriguing investments available for your IRA, including real estate, stocks and bonds of privately owned companies, private jet leasing, race horses, oil wells, gold, silver, platinum, palladium bullion (whatever that is), stock options, or even bull semen, which may not seem particularly savory to you, but to a cattle breeder is worth its weight in palladium.

Ever the spoil sport, however, the IRS will not let you invest your IRA funds in life insurance policies, arts, rugs, antiques, stamps, coins, or alcoholic beverages.

The key to any of these unusual IRA investments is a self-directed IRA, through which you choose the particular investments involved. With a more conventional IRA, you pick mutual funds through a custodian, be it a bank or a brokerage house. Although you may choose the particular mutual fund, you do not pick the individual stocks that make up the fund. There's nothing wrong with this kind of investing. In fact, investing inside or outside an IRA in low-cost index mutual funds has proven to be an effective strategy for successful long-term growth.

Subject, of course, to some rules and limitations of the IRS, there is a world of intriguing investments available for your IRA.

With a self-directed IRA, you still are required to have a custodian hold the particular investment in your IRA on your behalf, but you take more control over the investment choices. Not every IRA custodian will work with you in a self-directed IRA, but plenty of them will, and you won't have difficulty locating a trustworthy custodian for your self-directed IRA.

Once you've found a custodian you're comfortable with, it is a simple matter to set up an account and direct the custodian to invest in your particular investment of choice.

As with any investment, there are potential pitfalls, which in the case of self-directed IRAs are magnified because of the humorless IRS's response when self-directed IRAs are not done in full compliance with IRS regulations. Unlike in the game Monopoly, you are not required to "go directly to jail," but you do face the real possibility of having the IRS disqualify your IRA, tax it retroactively at high ordinary income tax rates, and then impose a 10% early withdrawal penalty if you are under the magic age of 59 1/2. So, whether you are playing Monopoly or investing in a self-directed IRA, it is critical to play by the rules. Don't abuse a self-directed IRA by violating the IRS primary rule by using the investment for your own financial well-being outside of its value as an investment. For example, your self-directed IRA should not

- Invest in a company that you or a family member owns

- Buy a home for you or a family member to live in

- Lease assets to you or a family member

- Loan money to you or a family member

The IRS rules regarding self-dealing can be quite confusing, so the easiest choice is to merely avoid anything that even comes close. If it walks like a duck and quacks like a duck, your goose could be cooked by the IRS.

Another important thing to keep in mind if your self-directed IRA is traditional is that you are required to start taking distributions from your IRA once you reach the age of 70 1/2, so it is critical that any unconventional investment that you use to form the basis of your self-directed IRA be sufficiently liquid to permit you to do so without difficulty. If you violate this rule, the IRS penalizes you at a rate of 50% of what you should have withdrawn from your account as a Minimum Required Distribution but didn't. Fortunately, if you use a Roth IRA as the vehicle for your self-directed IRA, this rule won't apply to you, because no mandatory withdrawals are ever required by the original owner of a Roth IRA.

Just as it is a poor choice to put a tax-deferred annuity into an IRA because it is already tax deferred, so might the tax advantages of owning real estate outside of an IRA and disadvantages of owning it in a traditional IRA make real estate a less-than-stellar choice for an investment to be held in a self-directed traditional IRA. The profit on the sale of investment real estate, such as commercial real estate when sold by someone outside of an IRA, is subject to the low 15% maximum federal income tax rate on long-term capital gains. However, if that same real estate is held in a self-directed traditional IRA, although there would be no immediate income taxes due when the real estate were sold by the self-directed IRA, once the IRA owner starts to distribute the income from that sale, the income tax rate that would apply would be at higher ordinary income tax rates. Profits from real estate held in a self-directed Roth IRA could be distributed tax free. However, real estate held in either a self-directed traditional IRA or a self-directed Roth IRA is not eligible for either the mortgage interest and real estate tax deductions or depreciation.

> **Real estate held in either a self-directed traditional IRA or a self-directed Roth IRA is not eligible for either the mortgage interest and real estate tax deductions or depreciation.**

Another problem with real estate in a self-directed traditional IRA occurs if you die while the real estate is still in your self-directed traditional IRA. In that situation, your heirs would not receive a step up in basis of the real estate. For example, if you bought a commercial building in your self-directed traditional IRA for $300,000 that was worth $600,000 at the time of your death, your heirs would pay income taxes on the gain as it is distributed at high ordinary income tax rates. However, if you had owned the same building personally outside of an IRA, your heirs who inherited the building at its $600,000 value would pay no income tax if they sold the inherited building after your death.

TRUTH

14

Stretch IRA

An IRA, be it traditional or Roth, can provide a tremendous opportunity to take advantage of the tremendous wealth-building benefits of tax-deferred or, in the case of a Roth IRA, tax-free compounded growth. It is an undeniable fact that the longer your money grows undisturbed by taxes, the greater the growth will be.

So enter the Stretch IRA.

Many people who have saved tremendous amounts of money in their IRAs do not spend the money during their lifetime. Owners of traditional IRAs can put off taking distributions from their IRAs until they attain the age of 70 1/2. Federal law determines the amount that investors must take each year from their IRAs. This is described as the Minimum Required Distribution amount, and it represents the IRS's calculations as to how much you need to take to completely use up the IRA during your lifetime. But the IRS's calculations are nothing more than educated guesses as to how long you will live. Many people die while still owning substantial amounts of money in their traditional IRAs, which, if handled appropriately through a Stretch IRA, can provide many years more of tax deferral for their spouses, children, grandchildren, or whomever they want to give their IRA to at death.

> It is an undeniable fact that the longer your money grows undisturbed by taxes, the greater the growth will be.

Owners of Roth IRAs are not required to take distributions from their Roth IRAs during their lifetime. They can let the money in their Roth IRAs continue to compound and grow entirely free of income taxes and then, at death, if they utilize a Stretch IRA, provide for the continuing tax-free growth of their Roth IRA for the benefit of their spouses, children, grandchildren, or anyone else they want to benefit from their wise planning.

What's the catch?

There isn't any.

The first step in being able to take advantage of a Stretch IRA is the proper completion of your Beneficiary Designation. The owner of an IRA is the initial beneficiary of the IRA. However, at death, the beneficiary designation form controls where the funds in the IRA will go next. For example, Homer has an IRA in which he names his wife Marge as his primary beneficiary. She is the first person in line to receive Homer's IRA at his death. Homer also, however, can list Lisa, Bart, and Maggie as equal secondary beneficiaries of his IRA such that if Marge either predeceases Homer or decides not to take the IRA money that she has a right to but disclaims the money, the IRA passes to Lisa, Bart, and Maggie. If Marge decides to take all of Homer's IRA, she can roll over Homer's IRA into her own IRA and, if the IRA is a traditional IRA, continue to defer taxes until she reaches the age of 70 1/2. She also, of course, has the option of taking whatever she wants from the account without penalty, although subject to income tax if Marge is over the age of 59 1/2.

If, on the other hand, Homer wisely had picked a Roth IRA as his IRA of choice, then upon his death, Marge would have the option of rolling the funds in Homer's IRA into a Roth IRA for herself. At that point, she could choose to take whatever amounts she wanted tax free or, more interestingly, allow the money in her Roth IRA to grow and compound for hopefully many more years tax free, at which point she could pass on the IRA to Lisa, Bart, and Maggie, who are her beneficiaries.

Regardless of when Lisa, Bart, and Maggie inherit the IRA, whether at the death of Homer or at the death of Marge, they can have the money transferred to an inherited IRA, under the terms of which they will be permitted to continue tax-deferred or tax-free growth, based on whether the IRA they are inheriting is a traditional IRA or a Roth IRA. The period they are allowed to continue the tax-deferred or tax-free growth is based on IRS determinations of their life expectancies, as indicated in a simple IRS table. Unlike the situation if Marge inherits a Roth IRA from Homer, if the children inherit the Roth IRA from Homer, they are required to take annual distributions. However, these annual distributions are based on their IRS-determined life expectancies, so the tax-free compound growth provided in a Roth IRA can continue, most likely for many years.

Let's look at what this means.

If Marge were to disclaim her interest in Homer's IRA and Maggie, as a one-year-old, were to receive $50,000 from Homer's IRA, she would have to take minimum required distributions over her projected life expectancy of 81.6 years. In the first year, Maggie would be required to take only $612.75 from the inherited IRA and permit the rest of it to grow on either a tax-deferred (if the IRA was a traditional IRA) or a tax-free basis (if the IRA was a Roth IRA). Traditionally, the stock market has averaged 10% per year, with some years earning substantially more and some years earning substantially less. However, even if you assumed a more conservative but entirely realistic 8% return on the fund invested in the IRA, after 81.6 years, Maggie would have received a total of $4,083,810. If the IRA had been a traditional IRA, she would have had to pay income taxes on the money she received each year, but if the IRA had been a Roth IRA, the entire $4,083,810 she received would have been totally income tax free.

> The key to a Stretch IRA is that the Beneficiary Designation must have the proper designations in place.

The key to a Stretch IRA is that the Beneficiary Designation must have the proper designations in place. If the Beneficiary Designation in the previous example did not specifically indicate Maggie as a beneficiary or if the beneficiary as designated was the estate of Homer Simpson, the benefits of the Stretch IRA would be lost, and the funds would be required to come out of Homer's IRA in no more than five years.

The lesson here is to always make sure that your Beneficiary Designation is in proper order to provide for a Stretch IRA.

TRUTH

15

Disclaimers

Perhaps Nancy Reagan was right when she proclaimed, "Just say no." She was talking about staying away from drugs, but her advice is just as valuable when it refers to the ability to use the financial and estate-planning tool known as a disclaimer.

A Disclaimer is a written refusal to accept assets that you become entitled to. It can, for instance, apply to the beneficiary of a life insurance policy, a bequest in a will, or even inheritance of a 401(k) or IRA. When you disclaim what you would receive as the designated beneficiary of a 401(k) or an IRA, the 401(k) or IRA then passes to the beneficiary designated next on the beneficiary designation form of the owner of the 401(k) or IRA.

The beauty of a Disclaimer is that it allows you to change your estate plan after you've died. In effect, it allows you to change your bet on the race after it's over. For example, as is commonly done, you may name your spouse as the beneficiary of your IRA. If you die, the remaining money in your IRA can be rolled over into your spouse's IRA. However, your spouse may already have enough money to meet her needs, or she may not want to add more assets to her estate that could possibly make her estate subject to estate taxes when she dies.

If a proper beneficiary designation is in place that names not just the surviving spouse as the primary beneficiary, but also, for example, the IRA owner's children as secondary beneficiaries, the surviving spouse is now in the position to be able to disclaim or renounce the IRA that she would be entitled to, in which case, it would pass to the children as the next named beneficiaries. If there were three children who were ages 25, 27, and 29, they would then be in a position to establish inherited IRAs and stretch out the tax deferral of their receipt of the funds from a traditional IRA over the next 58.2, 56.2, and 54.3 years respectively. To make things even better, if the children were the designated secondary beneficiaries of a Roth IRA

> **The beauty of a Disclaimer is that it allows you to change your estate plan after you've died.**

that they received through the use of a qualified Disclaimer, they would still be required to take the money out of the inherited IRA over the same number of years, but this time they would pay absolutely no income tax on any of the money they were required to withdraw from the inherited IRAs, continuing the tax-free compounding of the original Roth IRA investments for more than half a century.

The key to being able to effectively disclaim an inherited IRA or 401(k) is to have a proper Beneficiary Designation prepared by the original IRA owner

As good as this sounds, in reality it is even better. If, in the previous example, the surviving spouse decides that he wants or needs some of the money from his deceased spouse's IRA, he can claim whatever portion he wants and disclaim the rest. Thus, this makes planning for the division of the IRA assets flexible and adaptable to the specific needs of the family at the time of the death of the original IRA owner.

The key to being able to effectively disclaim an inherited IRA or 401(k) is to have a proper Beneficiary Designation prepared by the original IRA owner who designates primary, secondary and perhaps even tertiary beneficiaries to provide for the utmost flexibility in disclaiming. So, for instance, if instead of having just the owner of the IRA name his spouse within the Beneficiary Designation as the primary beneficiary and his children as secondary beneficiaries, he also named his grandchildren or trusts on their behalf as tertiary beneficiaries, it is possible for any or all of the children to, in turn, disclaim their beneficial interest after their parent had disclaimed an interest that passed the property to them, in which case the IRA or a portion of it would pass to grandchildren. While a 25-year-old can continue tax-deferred compounding of a traditional IRA over the next 58.2 years, a 2-year-old grandchild inheriting the traditional IRA can continue tax-deferred compounding over the next 80.6 years. However, it is critical to remember that taking advantage of the potential benefits of a Stretch IRA requires that a proper beneficiary designation document already be in existence to name the contingent beneficiaries. Otherwise, you run the risk of needing to have the IRA funds come out of the IRA in as little as five years and lose the benefits of many years of either tax-deferred or even tax-free (in the case of a Roth IRA) compound growth.

There are a few rules that pertain to the use of Disclaimers. First, the Disclaimer must be in writing. Second and most importantly, the Disclaimer must be executed and delivered to the trustee of the 401(k) or IRA within nine months of the death of the 401(k) or IRA owner. Third, the person disclaiming cannot have taken possession of any of the 401(k) or IRA before disclaiming.

TIP Disclaiming is easy to do, but what if you are not competent? What if, for example, the surviving spouse, who has no need or desire to inherit the IRA of her spouse, is incompetent? In that case, the ability to execute a valid disclaimer would be lost unless the surviving spouse had a *Durable Power of Attorney*, a document by which the surviving spouse named someone to make financial decisions on her behalf if she were incompetent. A Durable Power of Attorney should be a part of everyone's financial and estate planning.

TRUTH

16

Inheriting an IRA

It always helps to know the rules. However, when it comes to inheriting an IRA, the rules can be so complicated that knowing them is just the start of knowing what to do. A surviving spouse inheriting an IRA is treated differently from anyone else inheriting an IRA. There are three possible situations that apply to a surviving spouse who is named the beneficiary of her deceased spouse's IRA.

Inheriting a traditional IRA from a deceased spouse who had not yet turned 70 1/2

The first situation occurs when you inherit an IRA from a deceased spouse who had not yet turned 70 1/2, the age at which minimum withdrawals must begin from a traditional IRA. Actually, believe it or not, the unnecessarily confusing federal rules state that if your spouse died before the April Fools Day of the year he would have turned 70 1/2, you can roll over the IRA into your own traditional IRA and keep on deferring taxes, if you so choose, until you reach the age of 70 1/2.

A surviving spouse inheriting an IRA is treated differently from anyone else inheriting an IRA.

Tricky alternative for a spouse inheriting a traditional IRA

If you are over the age of 70 1/2, you can keep the traditional IRA in the name of your deceased spouse until the year he would have turned 70 1/2 and continue to let the traditional IRA grow tax deferred. Of course, if you want or need to take any money from the IRA, you are free to do so, but the longer you leave the money in the traditional IRA, the more it grows and the longer you defer paying income taxes.

Inheriting a traditional IRA from a spouse over the age of 70 1/2

Again, technically this applies when you inherit a traditional IRA on or after April Fools Day of the year after your late spouse reached the age of 70 1/2. I would love to know what genius congressperson or senator came up with that date. As in the first situation, where you inherit the traditional IRA from a spouse who was under the age of 70 1/2, again you have the option of rolling the money over into your own traditional IRA. However, you first have to take out your deceased spouse's minimum required distribution for the year in which he died before you roll over his traditional IRA to your own.

You also have the option of leaving the account in your deceased spouse's name, but if you do so, you are required to take out larger minimum distributions, so this is never a good option.

Disclaiming a traditional IRA

The third situation that applies when a deceased spouse is named as the primary beneficiary of the traditional IRA of her deceased spouse is when the surviving spouse for whatever reasons decides that she does not want some or all of the money in the traditional IRA. In that situation, the surviving spouse can execute a disclaimer of whatever amount of the traditional IRA she does not want to take, and that amount disclaimed passes to whoever is designated as a contingent beneficiary on the Beneficiary Designation Form of the deceased owner of the traditional IRA.

There are many reasons why a person may choose to disclaim money that she would otherwise inherit from a deceased spouse's traditional IRA. The surviving spouse may believe that she has enough money, and by allowing the money to pass through a disclaimer to the next-in-line beneficiary, who often is a child or grandchild of the surviving spouse, she is able to, in essence, make a gift without gift tax ramifications. In addition, an older surviving spouse may want to reduce her assets to avoid possible estate taxes or having the assets disqualify her if in the future she may have to apply for Medicaid to pay for long-term care in a nursing home. If a surviving spouse had inherited the IRA and then made a gift of the money to her children or grandchildren, there would be a disqualification of as long as five years if she applied for Medicaid in the future. Having the traditional IRA money pass by way of a disclaimer to the same children or grandchildren would avoid any future Medicaid disqualification.

Nonspouse inheritance of a traditional IRA

When children, grandchildren, or anyone else inherits a traditional IRA, either directly or through a disclaimer, the options are more limited than those for a surviving spouse. Anyone other than a surviving spouse who inherits a traditional IRA must have the deceased person's IRA transferred to an inherited IRA that must be properly titled, such as "Homer Simpson, deceased, inherited IRA for the benefit of Lisa Simpson," and the beneficiary must take out minimum required distributions based on the age of the beneficiary. In this example, for instance, if Lisa Simpson were 12 years old, she would be required to take minimum required distributions based on her life expectancy, which for the first year would be 70.8 years. So if she were to inherit an IRA valued at $50,000, her initial minimum required distribution would be $706.21, thereby allowing considerable tax-deferred compounding of the inherited IRA.

Inheriting a Roth IRA

Because the owner of a Roth IRA is not required at any age to take mandatory distributions from her IRA, a spouse inheriting a Roth IRA does not have to concern herself with the age of her deceased spouse at the time of his death. The surviving spouse can either decide to roll over the Roth IRA into her own Roth IRA and take or not take distributions as she wants or she can disclaim all or some of the Roth IRA, in which case whatever amounts she disclaims pass to the contingent beneficiaries, who most likely are her children or grandchildren.

People other than a surviving spouse who inherit a Roth IRA must put the money into a specifically titled inherited Roth IRA, from which they must withdraw minimum required distributions each year. Fortunately, however, the required minimum distributions are based on the age of the person inheriting the Roth IRA, so for instance, a 30-year-old child who inherits a Roth IRA can spread out his minimum required distributions over the next 53.3 years and extend the tax-free compounding growth of the IRA.

TRUTH

17

Maximizing IRA benefits for a surviving spouse

Ours is a society where a premium is put on multitasking. People talk on the phone while doing paperwork. When it comes to IRAs, proper multitasking can provide for passing an IRA from a married person to his spouse at death and continuing income tax deferral while deferring estate taxes and preserving funds to be available for children at the death of the surviving spouse. Now that is a lot of multitasking!

Generally, passing an IRA from the holder of the IRA to a surviving spouse is a relatively easy task to accomplish. The key thing is to plan in advance by naming the spouse as the primary beneficiary. If the deceased IRA owner had not named the spouse as the beneficiary of the IRA, the surviving spouse still might be able to inherit the IRA if it passed to the deceased spouse's estate and through her will to the surviving spouse; however, the ability to defer income taxes beyond a period of five years would be lost.

Passing an IRA to a surviving spouse through a will would not necessarily provide for deferral of estate taxes and preserve assets for the children of the deceased IRA owner. To achieve those objectives, intricate planning involving trusts and the rules regarding Minimum Required Distribution is required. Federal estate tax law provides for an unlimited marital deduction, which means that any amount of assets left by a spouse at death to his surviving spouse will not be subject to estate taxes at the death of the initial spouse. This provides for a deferral of estate taxes until the death of the surviving spouse.

To qualify for the unlimited marital deduction, the surviving spouse generally must have total control over the assets left to him. In the case of an IRA, where you may want to provide for your surviving spouse but also ensure that the funds will not be depleted by the surviving spouse before passing at her death to children of the original IRA owner, a trust is necessary to achieve that goal. A Qualified Terminable Interest Property trust, which is more often referred to by the clever acronym QTIP, is a form of trust that provides an exception to the rule that, to qualify for the marital deduction, the surviving spouse must control the assets inherited from the deceased spouse. So long as the surviving spouse is the sole lifetime beneficiary of the QTIP trust and he receives at least all the trust income during his lifetime, the trust will qualify for the estate tax marital deduction and provide a valuable deferral of estate taxes.

A QTIP trust is most favored when the holder of an IRA wants the IRA to be used for the benefit of her surviving spouse but also wants to preserve a substantial part of the IRA for children of a previous marriage.

Now comes the next set of complications. When a trust is an IRA beneficiary, the Minimum Required Distribution amounts are determined by the age of the oldest trust beneficiary, which in the case of a QTIP trust is generally

A QTIP trust is most favored when the holder of an IRA wants the IRA to be used for the benefit of her surviving spouse but also wants to preserve a substantial part of the IRA for children of a previous marriage.

the surviving spouse. For example, if Marge is the beneficiary of a QTIP trust that receives the IRA of Homer following his death and Marge, at age 47, is the oldest beneficiary of the trust (Bart, Lisa, and Maggie, the secondary beneficiaries, are all younger), the appropriate IRS Single Life Expectancy Table indicates that Marge has a life expectancy of 37 years. Therefore, in the first year of the trust, the trustee must distribute to the trust 1/37 of the total account value of the IRA to satisfy the Minimum Required Distribution rules. Then all income of the trust must, in turn, be distributed to Marge, so the trust complies with the QTIP marital deduction estate tax rules.

A problem arises when determining the amount of the income to be distributed from the QTIP trust to Marge. According to the Uniform Principal and Income Act, which most states have adopted, the amount of income that an income beneficiary of a trust is entitled to is only 10% of a Minimum Required Distribution amount. If the amount that had to be withdrawn from Homer's IRA based on Marge's age was $100,000, the amount that the QTIP trust would actually distribute to Marge would be only $10,000, which not only would frustrate Marge but also would irritate the IRS. Such a small distribution amount from the IRA would not be characterized by the

IRS as a spousal bequest. Consequently, the marital deduction would not apply, and the estate of Homer would not be able to defer estate taxes through the use of the marital deduction and the QTIP trust.

Fortunately, the IRS has given us some guidance through Revenue Ruling 2006-26, which offers three alternatives to comply with both the QTIP rules and the MRD rules. The first alternative is by having a provision of the trust that permits the trustee to adjust the amounts of the investment income and principal to achieve a more fair distribution. So even though the actual investment income might be at a rate of only 4%, the trustee can determine that it would be fairer to all the beneficiaries to adjust the value of the IRA income to a figure of 6%. This process could be repeated each year so long as Marge lived.

The second alternative is to use a unitrust definition of income, by which the trust defines income as a specific percentage of the value of the trust's assets each year. This, too, could be used to arrive at a figure that would comply with both the QTIP and MRD rules.

Finally, the IRS recognizes that the traditional standards for trust income in place before the passage of the Uniform Principal and Income Act can be used whereby investment income and dividends are counted as income in a manner that can, once again, comply with both the QTIP and MRD rules and preserve all the goals of our multitasker.

If all this seems a bit confusing to you, don't be alarmed. It is confusing, which is why it's good for you to use an experienced attorney when drafting a QTIP trust that will be the beneficiary of an IRA.

TRUTH

18

Roth IRA for children

Setting up a Roth IRA for a child is my favorite use of this type of IRA, which has so many good aspects to it. With any investment, the longer you let the money compound, particularly if that growth is tax free, the greater the amount that you can accumulate. A child who contributes the maximum $5,000 per year from the age of 7 to the age of 18 and then never makes another contribution to her Roth IRA for the next 42 years will have accumulated $2,407,723 at age 60 assuming an 8% rate of return on the investments. Let's see how to put this to work.

The requirements for a Roth IRA are the same for anyone. There is no minimum age for a person to establish a Roth IRA. The only requirements are that the individual has earned income of at least $5,000 to contribute the maximum (in 2008) amount of $5,000. A child earning less than the standard deduction amount of $5,450 will not be liable for income taxes on her earnings. In addition, children under the age of 18 who work for their parents are not required to pay either Social Security or Medicare taxes on their wages. In fact, the law specifically exempts children under the age of 21 from being responsible for Social Security or Medicare taxes for domestic work performed at their parents' home.

> **Opening a Roth IRA for a child is the ultimate win-win situation.**

In addition, the punitive Kiddie Tax that significantly restricts parents' ability to shift investment income from themselves to their children in a lower income tax bracket does not apply to wages that children earn. Paying a child a reasonable wage to perform common household chores need not affect the parents' ability to take a dependency exemption for the child.

The key to establishing a Roth IRA for a child is performing work and earning a wage that is reasonably related to the work that the child performs. Don't abuse the rules. Just pay the child a reasonable wage for the work performed. However, without abusing the rules, it is easy to see how parents could hire a child to perform household chores—such as mowing the lawn, shoveling the driveway, or washing dishes—and pay the child $5,000 a year. It is also important to follow IRS rules and provide the child with a W-2 form at the end of the year. In addition, the parents should file an income tax return on behalf of the child.

The age of 7, which I used in my example, is not without a basis. In a landmark case, Walter and Dorothy Eller hired their three children, the youngest of whom was only seven years old, to perform work for them at their mobile home parks in California. The Tax Court ruled in their favor that a child as young as 7 can perform substantial services that warrant payment of wages.

> It is not even necessary for the child to use her own earned money to fund her Roth IRA.

It is not even necessary for the child to use her own earned money to fund her Roth IRA. All that is required by law is that the child earned the amount of money used to fund the Roth IRA up to the 2008 maximum of $5,000. The actual money used to fund the child's Roth IRA can come from a gift from parents, grandparents, or wherever. A child with no other earnings between the ages of 7 and 18 could, however, fund her Roth IRA with her earnings without paying a nickel of federal income tax and having the entire amount grow tax free for as long as the child desired, although that may represent the one potential downside of the Roth IRA. The money is the child's, and if she unwisely decides to tap into that stash at any time, she has the right to do so. However, it is not hard to imagine a parent impressing upon a child the benefit of having that money be set aside for a secure future.

S IRA administrators refuse to set up Roth IRAs for children because as minors, they cannot be bound by the contracts that they make. Fortunately, however, many of the major brokerage firms and mutual fund families are more than happy to take your money and open a custodial IRA for a minor as long as a parent or guardian cosigns the documents as the child's guardian. Some brokerage houses even offer custodial IRAs for children with no minimum balance requirements and no annual maintenance fees. Others require a minimum balance of as little as $100, and still other brokerage houses provide custodial IRAs for children with no minimum balance, but with small annual maintenance fees. Charles Schwab & Co., for example, provides a custodial IRA with no account service fees and a minimum opening contribution of only $100. The account remains a custodial account until the child reaches the age of majority, which in most states is 18, at which time the account is turned over to the child.

Opening a Roth IRA for a child is the ultimate win-win situation. The child learns the responsibility of performing work for a reasonable wage while contributing to an investment that can help insure a secure future.

TRUTH

IRA conversions

For many people, a Roth IRA offers more benefits than a traditional IRA. Unfortunately, some of these people did not come to this conclusion until after they had established a traditional IRA. Fortunately, the law permits you to convert your traditional IRA to a Roth IRA. However, there are some conditions and repercussions of such a conversion.

To be eligible to convert a traditional IRA to a Roth IRA, your adjusted gross income must be no more than $100,000. This figure applies whether you are single or a married person filing a joint return. Oddly, married people who file separate income tax returns are not eligible to convert a traditional IRA to a Roth IRA.

The best time to convert a traditional IRA account to a Roth IRA account is when the economy is down and the value of your traditional IRA is reduced.

Converting to a Roth IRA is a good news, bad news situation. The good news is that once you have converted your traditional IRA into a Roth IRA, all the money in that account will grow tax free and can be either withdrawn by you whenever you want or passed on to your heirs who can then also withdraw the money without having to pay income taxes on their withdrawals. The bad news is that when you do convert your traditional IRA to a Roth IRA, you must pay income taxes on all the money you convert. More bad news is that if the stock market drops after you have made your conversion, you are left with a tax bill based on the value of the IRA at the time of the conversion, not at the time that you pay your income taxes. For example, if you converted a traditional IRA worth $10,000 at the time of the conversion, but the value of the IRA drops due to declines in the stock market to $6,000, if you are in the 28% tax bracket, you will pay an extra $1,128 in income taxes. Fortunately, you can reverse your conversion and convert the account again later if you find yourself in this unenviable position.

The best time to convert a traditional IRA account to a Roth IRA account is when the economy is down and the value of your traditional IRA is reduced. IRS regulations permit you to nullify an IRA conversion that you did earlier in the year right up until the time that your income tax return is due, which can be as late as October 15 if you utilize extensions. To undo an IRA conversion, you must have the funds put back into a traditional IRA. You must also attach an IRS Form 8606 to your federal income tax return. Once circumstances become more favorable for a conversion, you can again convert your traditional IRA to a Roth IRA. However, IRS regulations prevent you from doing so until the next tax year. If you do your conversion and reversion of conversion at the end of the calendar year, you must wait at least 30 days between the time you undo a Roth IRA conversion and the time that you convert it back to a Roth IRA.

If you convert a traditional IRA to a Roth IRA, make sure that you do not take possession of the funds in your IRA but have the funds transferred directly from one IRA trustee to another, so you avoid adverse income tax consequences.

If you are under the magic age of 59 1/2, don't use money from your traditional IRA to pay the income taxes due on the conversion to a Roth IRA. Any money that you take out of your traditional IRA to pay the resulting income taxes is considered an early withdrawal that results in your being assessed a 10% penalty by the IRS in addition to the income taxes you'll owe.

> There is no requirement that a conversion from a traditional IRA to a Roth IRA be done entirely in one year.

Another important consideration when converting a traditional IRA to a Roth IRA is that the amount of your traditional IRA that you choose to convert to a Roth IRA is added to your other taxable income for that year, which could put you in a higher tax bracket. The optimum amount to convert would be no more than the ceiling of your present income tax rate bracket so that the conversion does not push you into a higher income tax bracket. You also may want to do a Roth IRA conversion prior to your beginning to take Social Security benefits. Otherwise, the taxable income from the conversion may cause an increase in the amount of income taxes you owe on your Social Security benefits.

There is no requirement that a conversion from a traditional IRA to a Roth IRA be done entirely in one year. In fact, it may be prudent to spread out the amount that you convert over a number of years.

Loophole

Beginning in 2010, if your adjusted gross income is greater than $100,000, you may convert your traditional IRA to a Roth IRA. People who are ineligible to establish a Roth IRA because, for example, their income is greater than allowed by law ($110,000 for single people and $160,000 for married people filing a joint income tax return) may want to take advantage of the upcoming change in the law by establishing a traditional IRA and then converting it to a Roth IRA in 2010. In fact, the law provides a special incentive to people to convert traditional IRAs to Roth IRAs in 2010. For that year only, the taxable income derived from the conversion can be reported over the next two years' tax returns rather than having to be paid in one year.

If all this sounds too good to be true and you are wondering why Congress would possibly be so generous to us, the answer is a simple one. They did not intend to be generous. Their intention was to increase the number of people who would be eligible to convert a traditional IRA to a Roth IRA so that they could get their hands on the income taxes that people taking advantage of this conversion would have to pay.

TRUTH

20

SIMPLE IRA

The SIMPLE IRA is hard to overlook, and not just because the government has chosen to spell its name in all capital letters.

Actually, although a SIMPLE IRA is meant to be simple, the name itself is an acronym for Savings Incentive Match Plan for Employees. Unlike most IRAs, in which the decision to set one up is entirely the choice of the individual, a SIMPLE IRA is an employer-sponsored retirement plan where, similar to a 401(k), contributions may be made by both the employer and the employee. As with a 401(k), however, the choice of whether or not to participate in an employer-sponsored SIMPLE IRA is that of the employee.

SIMPLE IRAs, are, as you might imagine, simpler (no surprise there) and less costly for an employer to put into place. The administrative costs involved are usually lower than other, more complex plans. Often it takes little more than a phone call to a sponsoring financial institution to get things rolling. The IRS has issued two model forms (Form 5305-SIMPLE and Form 5304-SIMPLE) that can be used to economically set up a SIMPLE IRA plan. Many banks and mutual funds have their own IRS approved forms. Federal law limits the availability of SIMPLE IRAs to companies that have no other retirement plan in effect and have no more than 100 employees. Under the terms of a SIMPLE IRA, the employer can

For small and startup companies, a SIMPLE IRA is a good choice for a low-cost, initial retirement plan.

either make matching employee contributions to the SIMPLE IRAs of employees who elect to participate in the program and have some of their salaries paid to their SIMPLE IRA account through a payroll deduction, or contribute a fixed percentage to all eligible employees. If an employer chooses to make payments that are not related to contributions made by the employee, the employer must contribute 2% of the employee's annual compensation to the SIMPLE IRA account of each employee. Matching contributions are on a dollar-for-dollar basis up to a maximum 3% of the employee's compensation. The choice of the percentage match is up to the employer, although the match must be at least 1%. When computing the percentage of compensation that the employee may contribute, or the amount of the employer's matching or nonmatching contribution, any wages or other compensation of the employee greater than $225,000 is ignored.

To be eligible to participate in a SIMPLE IRA program at work, an employee must have been employed by the company for at least one year and must be being paid at least $5,000 per year, although the employer has the option of reducing the level of the compensation requirement. Even a self-employed individual may qualify for a SIMPLE IRA.

Similar to a traditional IRA and a traditional 401(k), the money in a SIMPLE IRA grows on a tax-deferred basis. The amount that you can contribute to your SIMPLE IRA is limited in 2008 to $10,500, which is more than what you can contribute to a traditional IRA or Roth IRA and less than what you could contribute

> Similar to a traditional IRA and a traditional 401(k), the money in a SIMPLE IRA grows on a tax-deferred basis.

to a traditional 401(k). In addition, as with a traditional IRA and a traditional 401 (k), the SIMPLE IRA provides for employees who are at least 50 years old to be able to make a catch-up contribution to their SIMPLE IRA if their employer's plan permits such additional contributions. In 2008, the amount of the catch-up contribution is $2,500.

Unlike a traditional 401(k) where you may not be fully vested in all the money in your account until a specific period of time has elapsed, with a SIMPLE IRA, you are always fully vested in all the money, including any employer contributions. An employee who leaves her job may take her SIMPLE IRA and roll it over tax free to another SIMPLE IRA if her new employer sponsors a SIMPLE IRA plan. However, if the new employer does not have a SIMPLE IRA plan, the employee leaving a job can only roll over her SIMPLE IRA into a traditional IRA on a tax-free basis if the employee had been with the previous company's SIMPLE IRA program for at least two years.

As with traditional IRAs, the same early withdrawal 10% penalty applies, although the same exceptions to the early withdrawal penalty also apply. In addition, however, the penalty increases to

25% for early withdrawals from a SIMPLE IRA within the first two years of an employee's participation in the plan.

For small and startup companies, a SIMPLE IRA is a good choice for a low-cost, initial retirement plan.

TRUTH

SEP IRA

More than 20 million Americans are self-employed, and this number continues to grow. The rate of increase in self-employed businesses was more than 25% in the past six years, which is triple the growth rate of other types of businesses. There are many advantages to being self-employed, but there are certainly many challenges as well. Retirement planning for the self-employed is one of those challenges. To the rescue came Congress, which, in 1978, a mere four years after the initial IRA legislation was passed, created the SEP IRA, a retirement benefit aimed particularly at the needs of the self-employed.

Due to its relative simplicity of form and substance, the SEP IRA is ideal for a self-employed businessperson who wants to make a greater tax-advantaged contribution toward retirement than what would otherwise be available to him. In 2008, generally, the lesser of 25% of the employee's compensation or $46,000 could be contributed to a SEP IRA. Although SEP IRAs were primarily intended to help self-employed people save for retirement, they are also available to small businesses that have employees.

Although the rules and regulations pertaining to SEP IRAs, for the most part, are simple, the actual calculation of the amount that you may contribute to a SEP IRA can be a little complicated. If your business is organized as a corporation that pays you a salary reported on a W-2, the amount of your contribution can be as much as 25% of your salary up to the $46,000 limit in 2008. These contributions are fully tax deductible by the corporation.

Due to its relative simplicity of form and substance, the SEP IRA is ideal for a self-employed businessperson.

If, however, your business is organized as a sole proprietorship, a partnership, or a limited liability, your contributions to a SEP IRA may be up to 20% of your net adjusted self-employment income (derived by subtracting from your business income one-half of your self-employment tax) or net adjusted business profits up to the $46,000 maximum again.

The maximum amount that you can contribute to a SEP IRA compares favorably to the maximum amounts that you can contribute to other retirement plans available:

Traditional IRA	$5,000
Roth IRA	$5,000
SIMPLE IRA	$10,500
SIMPLE 401(K)	$10,500

Picky little detail

Unlike traditional IRAs, Roth IRAs, SIMPLE 401(k)s, and SIMPLE IRAs, the law makes no provision for additional catch-up contributions in SEP IRAs by people 50 and over.

Also, as with other types of IRAs, you are not allowed to borrow money from your SEP IRA as you may with a 401(k).

Similar also to the SIMPLE IRA and SIMPLE 401(k), all the money contained in a SEP IRA is immediately vested in the employee. This is not important if you are self-employed, since you would control this money in any event, but it may be significant if you have a few employees and are concerned with providing an incentive to employees to stay with the company, incentives such as exist with retirement programs that contain delayed vesting provisions.

Flexibility is a hallmark of the SEP IRA. You are not required to make payments on an annual basis, which is an important consideration if you have employees and are concerned about the cash flow required to fund the program on a regular basis. Payments to the SEP IRA come totally from the employer, which again, is not significant if you are self-employed and have no other employees, but it may be an important concern if you have employees.

Employees who have worked at least three of the preceding five years with the company and earned a minimum of $500 a year must be covered by the company SEP IRA plan. This doesn't mean anything if you are a sole proprietor, but if you have other employees who meet this liberal qualifying requirement, you are obligated to cover them in the plan. One way to make this provision particularly work to your family's advantage is to hire your spouse and children to work for the company, in which case you could open SEP IRAs for each of them. But remember not to abuse the rules. If you are going to hire family members to work for your company, make sure they actually perform services and are not paid an excessive amount for their labor.

SEP IRAs also offer the self-employed person more time to fund the SEP IRA each year. Contributions to a SEP IRA are not required until the company's, or if the business is organized as a sole proprietorship, the individual owner's tax-filing deadline, including extensions. Therefore, unlike the funding of a traditional IRA or a Roth IRA, which must be done by the April 15 tax filing deadline each year, the funding of a SEP IRA may be delayed until the time of any extensions allowed for filing, which can be as late as October 15. Of course, as always, the earlier in the year that you fund any tax-deferred retirement investment, the sooner this money is working for you. But it is still nice to have this additional flexibility, particularly if you are self-employed and waiting to see what you can afford to put into your SEP IRA.

Similar to individual traditional IRAs, the contributions of an individual to a SEP IRA grow tax deferred and must begin to be withdrawn at age 70 1/2. Note that the rules for early withdrawals from traditional IRAs also apply to SEP IRAs.

Setting up a SEP IRA plan for yourself or your business if you have other employees is extremely simple and inexpensive. All the employer has to do is complete a simple IRS Form 5305-SEP. Each employee completes his own IRA application and makes his own investment decisions for his individual SEP IRA account. The choice of investments is as broad as with any traditional IRA.

For a self-employed person who may or may not have a few employees, retirement saving does not get much easier than the SEP IRA.

TRUTH

IRA effects on taxation of Social Security benefits

Tax planning doesn't end once you are retired. Social Security benefits that you receive may be subject to income tax. Yet, with a bit of planning, you can avoid or reduce the potential tax bite into your Social Security retirement benefits.

Whether you will have to pay income tax on payments that you receive from Social Security depends on your Provisional Income. The concept of *Provisional Income* is found only in the Internal Revenue Code. It is defined as the amount of your income determined by adding half of your net Social Security benefits and the amounts of some of your tax-exempt sources of income, such as tax-exempt municipal bonds to your taxable income.

If you are married and file a joint tax return, none of your net Social Security retirement benefits are taxable if your Provisional Income is no greater than $32,000. If you are single or file as married filing separately or as a head of household, you are subject to income tax on the amount of your Provisional Income that exceeds $25,000. It is particularly important to determine whether the amount of your Provisional Income will make you subject to additional income taxes, because if you have not accounted for this in your income tax withholding, if you are still working, or in your estimated tax payments, you could find yourself subject to a nasty penalty for underpayment of taxes.

For you gamblers out there, your winnings could play a part in making your Social Security benefits subject to income tax. Many people mistakenly believe that they only have to report as taxable income the amount of their winnings after deducting the amount of their losses for the year, but this is not accurate. The truth is that all your gambling winnings are counted toward the determination

> Whether you will have to pay income tax on payments that you receive from Social Security depends on your provisional income.

of your Provisional Income. Although you are allowed to deduct your gambling losses, you are only allowed to do so if you itemize your deductions and do not take the standard deduction. In any event,

whether you itemize your deductions, the entire amount of your
gambling winnings for the year is included in your Provisional Income

If your Provisional Income is
more than $32,000 but not greater
than $44,000 and you file a joint
income tax return with your spouse,
up to half of your Social Security
retirement benefits will be subject
to income tax. If your Provisional
Income is more than $25,000 and
no greater than $34,000 and you
are filing singly or married filing
separately, up to half of your Social
Security benefits will be subject to
income tax.

**This increase
in your taxable
income also puts
you in jeopardy of
going into a higher
income tax bracket
so that the rate of
your income tax
increases.**

If, on the other hand, your Provisional Income is more than
$44,000 and you file a joint income tax return with your spouse,
as much as 85% of your Social Security retirement benefits could
be subject to income taxes. If your provisional income is more than
$34,000 and you are filing singly or married filing separately, you too
may have as much as 85% of your Social Security retirement benefits
subject to income taxes.

To add even more woe to your situation, this increase in your
taxable income also puts you in jeopardy of going into a higher
income tax bracket so that the rate of your income tax increases.

But, finally, some good news.

In determining your Provisional Income, any distributions that you
take from your Roth IRA are not only tax-free, but they also are not
used in the determination of your Provisional Income. This is another
distinct advantage of a Roth IRA over a traditional IRA, because any
distributions that you receive from your traditional IRA are used in
the determination of your Provisional Income. If you have reached the
age of 70 1/2, annually you must take at least a minimum required
distribution from your traditional IRA, which is fully countable as
ordinary income for the calculation of your Provisional Income to
determine whether you will owe income taxes on your Social Security
retirement benefits.

To avoid this potential problem, you may want to consider converting your traditional IRA to a Roth IRA. However, once again, you must do your homework and make sure that the income taxes you are required to pay on the funds you convert from your traditional IRA to a Roth IRA do not put you into a higher income tax bracket. As always, the earlier you plan, the better. IRA conversions are not required to be done in a single year. You may find it advantageous to spread out your IRA conversion over a number of years to avoid raising of your income tax rate due to the income attributed to you when you convert.

Planning to do your conversion before age 70 1/2 not only permits more of your money to grow tax free in the Roth IRA, but it gives you more control over the amount of money that you convert in a particular year because you won't have reached the age of mandatory withdrawals. There are worksheets in IRS publication 915 that can assist you in determining whether your Social Security benefits will be subject to income tax and, if so, the amount of your Social Security benefits that will be subject to income taxes.

TRUTH

Excess contributions to a Roth IRA

Mae West used to say that too much of a good thing can be wonderful, but if you have made an excess contribution to a Roth IRA for which you did not qualify, it can create problems for you. Fortunately, this is one of the few places where the IRS readily permits you to have a mulligan, a do-over.

For you to make the maximum contribution to a Roth IRA in 2008, the IRS requires you to have at least $5,000 (or $6,000 if you are 50 years old or older) of earned income. That generally does not present much of a problem to anyone wishing to contribute to a Roth IRA. If you determine that you have sufficient income to qualify to contribute to a Roth IRA, the next step is to determine how much you can put into a Roth IRA. In 2008, the law limited the full $5,000 or $6,000 (if you are 50 or older) contributions to individuals who do not have more than $101,000 of income or married couples filing a joint income tax return with no more than $159,000 of income. However, if you are a single person with income between $101,000 and $116,000, the law permits you to make a partial contribution to a Roth IRA, while married couples filing jointly with income between $159,000 and $169,000 may also make a partial contribution to a Roth IRA. People eligible for a partial contribution to a Roth IRA can go to the Bible of IRAs, IRS Publication 590, for the 11-step calculation to see how much they may contribute.

It is possible for a person to take the excess contribution that she made to a Roth IRA and have that amount recharacterized as a contribution to a traditional IRA.

But what if you made a mistake and either miscalculated your income for the year or merely applied the rules improperly and ended up contributing more to a Roth IRA than the law will allow?

Fortunately, the law permits you to contribute to both a Roth IRA and a traditional IRA in the same year. The only requirement is that the total amount you contribute to your IRAs in a single year not exceed the maximum that can be contributed to IRAs in a single year, which, as I indicated earlier was $5,000, or $6,000 if you are 50 or over. So it is possible for a person to take the excess contribution that she made to a Roth IRA and have that amount recharacterized as a contribution to a traditional IRA. Of course, there are rules that must be followed precisely to take advantage of this opportunity. First and foremost is the requirement that the transfer from your Roth IRA to your traditional IRA be done as a trustee-to-trustee transfer. This means that you cannot personally take the excess contribution from your Roth IRA and send it to the trustee of your traditional IRA. Rather, you must instruct the trustee of your Roth IRA to send the money directly to the trustee of your traditional IRA.

> An IRA is still a good deal even if you can't take a deduction because of the valuable tax-deferred compound growth it provides.

As an additional bonus, if you make the trustee-to-trustee transfer of your excess contribution before October 15, you can treat the original contribution of the excess funds as if you had made the contribution directly to your traditional IRA for that previous tax year, which means that you may be eligible for an income tax deduction for the contribution. Tax-deductible contributions to a traditional IRA depend on your income, but the amount of your income that is counted in determining whether you are eligible to deduct your contribution to your traditional IRA is, in turn, dependent on whether you are covered by a qualified retirement plan at your place of employment. The easiest way to determine this is to look at your W-2 for the year and see if the box for Retirement Plan is checked. If the box is checked, you were covered by a qualified plan.

If you were single and covered by a retirement plan at work in 2008, you could deduct the full amount of your contribution if your income was no more than $53,000. If your income was between $53,000 and $63,000, you could deduct part of your contribution. If your income was more than $63,000, you were out of luck and could not t take a deduction on your income taxes for your contribution. If you are married and file a joint return, you may deduct the full amount of your contribution if your income is no more than $85,000. The deduction is phased out between $85,000 and $105,000 and is lost once your joint income reaches $105,000. Again, to compute the amount of any partial deduction you may be entitled to, go to IRS Publication 590.

If you do a recharacterization by taking excess money contributed to a Roth IRA and having it contributed to a traditional IRA, it is important that you not only transfer the amount of your excess earnings, but also the amount of any earnings attributable to your excess contribution while it was invested in your Roth IRA.

If you are ineligible to contribute to a traditional IRA because you have reached the magic age of 70 1/2 or if you just want the money, you can correct your excess contribution to your Roth IRA by merely removing your excess contribution from your Roth IRA without penalty. The reason that there is no penalty is that you made your initial Roth IRA contribution with money upon which you had already paid taxes, so your rich Uncle Sam lost nothing when you put it into your Roth IRA. However, unless you are at least 59 1/2 and have had your Roth IRA for at least five years, you will have to pay a 10% penalty as well as income taxes on any earnings that accrued from your excess contribution, although it is doubtful that this would amount to a substantial penalty since your excess contribution would have been in your Roth IRA for only a short time.

The one thing you absolutely should not do is ignore the situation and leave the excess contribution in your Roth IRA, because there is a 6% excise tax penalty on excess contributions.

TRUTH

24

401(k)

Although it may seem like it has always been around, Section 401(k) of the Internal Revenue Code was passed in 1978. For one of the most powerful retirement savings vehicles available today, it does not have a very fancy name. It did not even have a sponsor in Congress eager to have his name associated with it, as in the case of the Roth IRA. It is just the 401(k).

If the 401(k) did have a name associated with it, it would be that of Ted Benna, a man of incredible vision who was able to crack the Internal Revenue Code and turn an innocuous provision, 401(k), into the basis of a retirement revolution. In 1980, he used the law to set up the first pretax salary reduction, employee contribution, company match, retirement plan using provisions of IRC section 401(k) that had been missed by the rest of the financial planning world. The use of employee pretax contributions to fund a retirement account was entirely unforeseen when Congress passed the initial 401(k) law. Even the IRS was unprepared for Benna's innovation, but to the surprise of many, the IRS approved Benna's interpretation of the law, thereby setting the stage for a dramatic change in how American retirement plans are funded.

With the traditional defined benefit pension plan going the way of the dinosaur (who, by the way, had an awful retirement plan), the 401(k) has become the retirement plan of choice for most companies. The most common type of 401(k) plan is the traditional 401(k) plan, which is set up by the employer and permits individual employees to contribute a portion of their wages to a retirement plan before those wages have been subjected to income taxes. The money you contribute to your 401(k) account is neither subject to federal income tax withholding nor subject to income tax in the year that you contribute to your 401(k) account.

> There may be no free lunches, but there actually is free money in many traditional 401(k) accounts.

Once in your 401(k) account, your money grows in the investments of your choice from an array of investment options made available to you in your particular plan. These investments include stock mutual funds, bond funds, money market funds, and even stock in the company you work for. The growth of your investment is on a tax-deferred basis. No income tax is due until you withdraw the money from your 401(k). The money you contribute to your traditional 401(k) plan comes directly out of your paycheck as a payroll deduction, so once you have enrolled in your company's traditional 401(k) plan, it requires no effort to regularly save for retirement.

There may be no free lunches, but there actually is free money in many traditional 401(k) accounts. In an effort to induce their employees to save for retirement and to reward them for their service to the company, many companies provide matching contributions of as little as 10% or as much as 100% of the employee's contribution, depending on the terms of the particular company 401(k) plan.

> One of the major additional benefits of a 401(k) plan over an IRA is the considerably higher amount that an individual may contribute to his 401(k).

Some employers pay their matching contribution as either a specific percentage of the employee's wages or a method to make a profit sharing contribution. Employers are allowed to require a certain period of employment at the company before an employee is eligible for a matching contribution. In addition, as an inducement of employees to stay with their particular employer, the employer can provide in the particular terms of its company 401(k) plan that the matching contributions of the employer are not vested in the employee until after a particular period of time, commonly five years.

One of the major additional benefits of a 401(k) plan over an IRA is the considerably higher amount that an individual may contribute to his 401(k). While in 2008, the limit for contribution to an IRA was $5,000 for someone under the age of 50 and $6,000 for people 50 and over, the limit for contribution to a 401(k) is a much healthier $15,500 for those under 50. If you are 50 years old or older, you can contribute an additional $5,000, for a total maximum contribution of $20,500. The advantage is tremendous if you are able to put away that much more money to work for you on a tax-deferred basis.

When you leave your company, you have a number of decisions to make regarding your 401(k). You can do nothing and leave it with the company to continue growing, but without your being able to make additional contributions to the account. You also can choose to have your 401(k) plan transferred and rolled over into your 401(k) account with your new employer, if your new employer, as most do, offers a 401(k) plan. Another option available to you is to have the account rolled over into an IRA that you can self-direct. This option may not only provide you with a greater choice as to investment options for your retirement money, but also may be much less costly to you in regard to the maintenance fees related to your IRA as compared to your previous company's 401(k) plan fees.

The last option available to you when you leave a company is the one that should be used only as a last resort: Take the money out of the 401(k) plan without putting it into another retirement account. Unless you have reached the magic age of 59 1/2, if you utilize this option, not only will you be assessed income taxes on the money you take out of your 401(k) account, but you also will be subject to an additional 10% excise tax penalty for an early withdrawal unless certain exceptions apply, such as using the money to buy a home, avoid foreclosure on a home you already own, pay for certain education expenses, pay for uncovered medical expenses, pay for certain home repair expenses, or pay for funeral expenses for family members. Unfortunately, too many people just take the money from their 401(k) accounts and spend it. Not only will this subject you to immediate income taxes as well as the excise tax penalty if you are under 59 1/2, but it will also eliminate the future tax-deferred growth of your retirement investment.

TRUTH

401(k) fees

My mantra has always been that for any investment, it is not what you make that is important; it is what you keep. An investment that initially may appear to be quite profitable, may, in fact, be quite the opposite when you consider how fees can reduce the value of that investment.

An additional 1% of fees may not seem like much, but when you consider the double-edged sword represented by excessive fees that not only reduce the amount of your money working for you today but also take away the value of that money compounding through many tomorrows until your retirement, the effect can be tremendous. Additional 401(k) fees of a mere 1% over your working career can effectively reduce the amount that you have in your account at retirement by 28% or more.

> Additional 401(k) fees of a mere 1% over your working career can effectively reduce the amount that you have in your account at retirement by 28% or more.

The true shame of this loss of value by 401(k) participants is that often they are not even aware of the amount of fees they are paying.

According to Shakespeare, a rose by any other name would smell as sweet. When it comes to 401(k) plan fees, they are called by various names, but the cumulative effect is that many don't smell very good. It costs money to administer a 401(k) plan. Of that there is no dispute. In 1988, the vast majority of companies paid all the fees related to administering their 401(k) plans. Today, however, that number has dropped to 25%. And, although by federal law, employers are required to make sure that fees and expenses are kept at reasonable levels in relation to the services provided by the plan, this law has been honored as much in the breach as the observance.

The basic fee involved in a 401(k) plan is the plan administration fee, which covers the cost of the normal operating of the plan. This fee is intended to cover basic accounting, legal, and trustee services. However, the equivalent of "Do you want fries with that?" is the question of what other services are added to the basic plan that can, to unwary participants in the plan, add significantly to the administration fees that they pay. Certainly, education as to the investment alternatives and strategies that the plan offers is important, but the cost of seminars, investment advice, and retirement planning software can serve to raise the fees and lower the return on the accounts of individual 401(k) participants. Additional bells and whistles such as online transaction capabilities, investment advice, and 24-hour customer service sound attractive until you realize that someone has to pay for these services, and that someone is you. Do you really need to be able to talk to someone about your 401(k) account at 2:00 in the morning?

The largest fees, however, relate to management of the investments that make up the plan. Unfortunately, many of these fees are hidden and come in the form of indirect charges against your account that are deducted from your investment but are not readily disclosed so that, although your investment return is reduced by these fees, they are not sufficiently disclosed such that you would be aware of what you were paying. You also may be subject to particular fees that relate to specific services, such as taking a loan from your 401(k).

Additionally, within the mutual funds that make up the bulk of your investment options within your 401(k) plan are various sales charges that further serve to reduce the value of your account. Even if you choose a fund that says it is *no-load*, meaning it does not have sales charges either when you enter or leave the fund, you still may be charged 12b-1 fees, which represent fees you pay that subsidize the mutual fund company's advertising and promotional costs.

Most of the mutual funds contained in 401(k) plans are actively managed funds that are constantly trading stocks, monitoring the market, and doing considerable investment research, all of which costs money, yet does not, either in theory or in practice, provide better investment returns than passively managed index funds that have lower management fees. All too often, companies fail to include within their menu of investment options many choices of index mutual funds, which

> The largest fees, however, relate to management of the investments that make up the plan.

represent some of the most profitable and least costly investment options. Instead, companies tend to add actively managed mutual funds that carry substantially higher fees than index funds without providing superior performance. In fact, a study by the University of Illinois at Urbana Champaign concluded that when you consider the actual return on investment after fees are accounted for, index mutual funds beat actively managed funds by .72% per year, a particularly significant figure when you consider the value of this money saved compounding over time.

So where can you find out about the fees you are paying?

The first place to look is your plan's summary plan description (SPD), which describes how expenses are allocated among plan participants. You receive a copy of this when you join your company's plan. The next place to look is on your account statement. Unfortunately, however, although some of the fees you are paying may be apparent from your statement, hidden fees, particularly those involved with investment management, may be impossible to find. Finally, you can get a copy of your company's annual report (Form 5500), which contains information about fees and expenses paid by the plan. Here again, unfortunately you pay many fees that are not apparent from viewing this form.

Ultimately, the best course to follow is to join with other employees participating in the plan and ask your employer for a detailed analysis of the plan's fees. After all, your employer is under a federal mandate to maintain fees at a reasonable level, so it should be more than willing (whatever that means) to cooperate with you. You and your fellow employees may be surprised when you find out the total fees paid by participants in the plan. Once you are aware of what you are paying and what you are getting for what you pay, you will be in a better position to lobby your employer for more cost-effective choices.

TRUTH

26

IRA and 401(k)
investments 101

Introductory courses in college often carry the designation 101, as in Economics 101. Once you have made the important decision to invest in your own retirement in an IRA or a 401(k), your next job is to determine the investments that you will include in your retirement accounts. Knowing and, more importantly, following a few basic rules should make your investment decisions much more productive in the long haul. So here is IRA and 401(k) investments 101.

An essential element of any successful investing plan is asset allocation. Asset allocation in IRAs and 401(k)s involves apportioning your investment dollars among a variety of investments, generally stocks, bonds, and cash in the forms of mutual funds. How much you allocate to each of these segments depends on your individual tolerance for risk. How comfortable are you taking a risk on investing more in stock mutual funds that provide the possibility of greater returns on your investment dollars but also carry the possibility of losing value and costing you money? Your tolerance for risk is not necessarily related to your age, although the older you are, the less likely you are to invest aggressively, because the danger of making a wrong decision is magnified when you do not have many years to make up for an investment decision that with 20/20 hindsight turns out to be a poor choice.

Having more conservative investments outside of your IRA and 401(k) may provide you with the opportunity to be more aggressive in your IRA and 401(k) investments.

Your personality may make you more aggressive as an older investor or more conservative as a younger investor. There are no hard and fast stereotypes when it comes to investment styles. However, many women invest less aggressively (and quite often more productively) than men. Overly conservative investing is not a good thing when it comes to investing. During the past 20 years, stock mutual funds have provided gains that averaged 6% more per year than the gains obtained by investing in conservative money market funds. One of the mistakes that many

IRA and 401(k) investors make is being afraid of the stock market and putting too many of their retirement dollars in conservative money market funds. Money market funds have a place in your asset allocation as the cash portion of your portfolio, but they should not be the dominant segment of your portfolio.

There are a number of helpful rule of thumb formulas that can help you determine how much of your IRA dollars and 401(k) dollars should be in stock mutual funds and how much should be in more conservative fixed income investments such as bond mutual funds and money market funds. One common formula determines the amount of bonds and fixed income investments in your portfolio by multiplying your age by 80%, with the remainder of your investment portfolio being held in stocks. Using this formula, a 65-year-old woman should have 52% of her portfolio in bonds and 48% in stocks.

Once you have made this determination, you should rebalance your investment portfolio annually both to adjust to rises and falls in the stock market as well as adjust to your increasing age, all of which are inevitable. However, rebalancing every few months or continually trading in your retirement accounts chasing after the best returns rarely succeeds in doing anything other than just increasing the costs incurred in managing your account and ultimately lowering the long-term value of your account.

Many people are unsure of their own abilities to maintain a proper asset allocation in their IRAs and 401(k)s. For them, Target Mutual Funds are a good investment choice. A Target Fund does the work for you, and who doesn't like that?

The managers of target mutual funds invest your money based on when you plan to retire and regularly adjust the balance of your investment dollars between stocks and bonds. These funds offer convenience and the investment

Do not put more than 10% of your 401(k) investment in your company's stock.

knowledge of professional money managers. Nothing is without its flaws, however, and Target Mutual Funds are no exception. Because most Target Funds are mutual funds that are made up of a mixture of other mutual funds, you pay fees in each of the mutual funds that make up the portfolio of funds in your target fund as well as an overall fee for management of the target fund. It can be an expensive way to do your investing. Always remember the cardinal rule of investing: It is not what you make that is important; it is what you keep. Every fee that you pay reduces the value and growth of your retirement money.

Because fees can have such a significant effect on the value of your IRA and 401(k), a winning investment strategy is to utilize index mutual funds as the primary basis for your investments in your IRA and 401(k). Index mutual funds are made up of all the stocks in a particular index, such as the S & P 500. There are many other indexes that are used, including some that allow you to invest in foreign emerging markets, such as China and India. You will not do better than the general market with an index fund, however; because the management of an index fund is simplified, the fees are considerably less, and you come out the winner in the long run. No less an expert than Warren Buffett, one of the wealthiest men and most savvy investors in the world, has said, "A low-cost index fund is the most sensible equity investment for the great majority of investors."

It is also important to remember that when you are considering your asset allocation, you consider not just the money you have invested in your IRA and 401(k), but also how those investments relate to investments you have outside of your IRA and 401(k). Having more conservative investments outside of your IRA and 401(k) may provide you with the opportunity to be more aggressive in your IRA and 401(k) investments.

One final word about 401(k) investments in your company stock: As many Enron employees learned the hard way, do not put more than 10% of your 401(k) investment in your company's stock no matter how tempting it may be to invest in something you think you know well.

TRUTH

What to do if you don't like your 401(k) choices

Making the choice to contribute to a 401(k) account for your retirement is a relatively easy decision. But once you have made that decision, the harder question becomes where to allocate your 401(k) dollars.

If you invest too conservatively in money market funds and bond funds, you're liable to shortchange yourself as to the growth you need for a secure retirement. On the other hand, if you are too aggressive in your investment strategy (or lack of one), you can find yourself taking too much risk of losing money as you chase after the elusive best place to get the most bang for your bucks.

Fortunately, there are formulas you can use to determine a proper asset allocation that balances risk with safety. Generally, the older you are, the more such formulas tend toward conservative investments, because the danger to you of a risky investment failing is greater the closer you are to retirement.

And, as always, it is not what you earn that is important but what you get to keep. Fees can have a considerable effect on the ultimate success or failure of your retirement investments. Investments that eat away much of your investment dollars through excessive fees reduce the amount of money that is able to compound and grow over time in your 401(k) account. Unnecessary, excessive fees can easily reduce the value of your 401(k) at retirement by 20% or more.

If you invest too conservatively in money market funds and bond funds, you're liable to shortchange yourself as to the growth you need for a secure retirement.

Many people are familiar with these basic facts of 401(k) investing. Unfortunately, most people are unfamiliar with a dirty little secret of 401(k)s that can seriously affect the success of retirement investing plans: pay-to-play arrangements.

Pay-to-play arrangement fees are paid by mutual fund companies that want to get a piece of the huge fees for managing 401(k) accounts paid to consultants that companies use to recommend the particular mutual funds to be offered in the company's 401(k) plan.

Rarely is this kickback (the consultants prefer the phrase *revenue sharing payments*) disclosed to the companies using the services of these consultants, although the receipt of such kickbacks affects the recommendations of mutual funds to the companies sponsoring a 401(k) plan. A result of this pay-to-play arrangement is that consultants often end up recommending funds that do not present the best opportunity for you to successfully invest for your retirement but pay kickbacks to themselves and contribute to their own successful retirement. The funds they recommend may come with the double whammy of high fees and low return. Although this may seem improper, quite often it is perfectly legal so long as the consultant does not actually manage the company 401(k) plan but only recommends funds for inclusion in the plan.

> All too often the investment choices that you have within your 401(k) are not as good as what you could get outside the plan.

All too often the investment choices that you have within your 401(k) are not as good as what you could get outside the plan. So what can you do?

Do your own research and find mutual funds that have low fees and good earnings. Then ask your company to include them as an option in your company's 401(k) plan. Although your company probably does not run its own 401(k) plan, but rather outsources the job, it still has the last word as to what investment options will be available to you and the other participants in the plan. If enough employees request a particular mutual fund, you stand a good chance that your company will include it in your 401(k) plan. Don't be like Blanche Dubois in Tennessee Williams's classic play *A Streetcar Named Desire* and depend on the kindness of strangers. Don't just blindly accept the choices that are made available to you in your company 401(k) plan. Do some research on the investment choices you have. If you like the choices, pick the ones that suit you best. However, if you don't like the choices available to you, let your fellow employees know about your research and join together to ask your employer to include mutual funds in your plan that you think would be better suited to your investment objectives.

You should also look into whether your company plan offers a self-directed brokerage window by which you can control your 401(k) plan investments by making investments on your own through a broker. Generally, this services requires an additional fee, but this can more than be made up for with your greater control over the choices of your investments as well as a greater awareness of the fees you are paying.

If your company is not receptive to including funds that will present you with a greater opportunity for a less costly, greater yielding mutual fund or provide you with a self-directed window, you may wish to reconsider your retirement investing strategy. You may want to consider maxing out your traditional IRA or Roth IRA before investing in your company's 401(k). However, the lure of free matching funds that your employer may provided is hard to ignore. In that case, you may be better off making sure that you are doing the best you can with the investment choices available to you within your company's plan, but when it comes time to leave your employer, you may wish to carefully evaluate your choices in your new company's 401(k) before you decide to roll over your 401(k) funds from your previous employer into your new employer's plan. You may be better off rolling that money into an IRA that permits you to have total control over the investments within your IRA and provides much greater control over the fees that you will be paying.

Just like when you were in high school, it pays to do your homework. In fact, doing some research to learn which investments provide the best opportunities for your 401(k) money will prove more valuable to you than doing your high school history homework ever did.

TRUTH

Vesting rules for 401(k)s

Now that we have determined that it is beneficial to participate in a 401(k) plan at work, are there any limitations on your ability to participate in the plan? Your employer does have some leeway about how it handles 401(k) plans.

One of the most important rules regarding participation in your company's 401(k) plan is the threshold question of when you'll be eligible to invest in one. Not all plans permit you to participate in your company's plan immediately. The law permits the employer to defer your eligibility for as long as a year from the time that you join the company. In addition, not all employers make matching contributions to your individual 401(k) plan, although most do. Even those that do may have rules pertaining to when they will commence making matching contributions and when you will be fully entitled to those employer contributions.

If an employer, as most do, decides to make a matching contribution to the contribution you made as an employee, it is not required to match your contribution dollar for dollar. Instead, plans often provide that the employer will contribute a match of often between 25% and 50% of your contribution up to a certain level. For instance, your employer may contribute 50% of any contribution you make up to the first 6% of your salary. So, if your salary is $75,000 and you contributed at least $4,500 to your 401(k) account, you would be eligible for and receive a matching payment from your employer of $2,250. This is free money, and although you would think that no one in their right mind would give up free money, many people fail to avail themselves of this tremendous opportunity by not contributing the minimum amount to their 401(k) plan necessary to receive this free matching payment. Don't make this mistake.

One of the most important rules regarding participation in your company's 401(k) plan is the threshold question of when you'll be eligible to invest in one.

Vesting is an issue that is often misunderstood. It represents the date at which you become the full owner of all the assets in your 401(k) plan. Many people are familiar with restrictions that can limit complete vesting in their accounts for as long as six years; however, the truth is that you are immediately vested in your own contributions to your 401(k) plan and any income earned from your personal contributions to your 401(k). However, your employer, in an effort to encourage you to stay with the company, is allowed by federal law not to fully vest you in its employer matching contributions to your 401(k) account for a period of years.

There are two types of vesting: graded vesting and cliff vesting. In a graded vesting plan, you get the right to an increasing amount of your employer's matching contribution each year that you are with the company. For instance, your vested amount could increase by 20% each year you are with the

The vesting rules of your 401(k) plan are particularly important if you are considering leaving your job.

company after the first year, so that after five years you would be fully vested in your employer's matching contributions to your 401(k) account. Federal law permits employers to take as long as six years before you are fully vested through a graded vesting plan.

Alternatively, with cliff vesting, your ownership of your employer's matching contributions to your 401(k) account goes from nothing to full vesting after a specific period of time. Federal law sets the maximum amount of time by which your full vesting may be delayed in a cliff vesting program as three years, although your particular employer may choose to lower that period.

The vesting rules of your 401(k) plan are particularly important if you are considering leaving your job. It may be that a short delay in seeking new employment could have a significant effect on the amount of the money that you will be able to take with you.

If you do leave your employer, either before or after you have become fully vested in your employer's matching contributions, although the law permits you to roll over whatever funds you are entitled to of your 401(k) money from your previous employer to the 401(k) plan of your new employer, the law does not require your new employer to provide for rollovers from previous employers into their plans. In this instance, you would always have the option of transferring the money to an IRA, leaving it with your former employer's 401(k) plan, or taking it out and paying the income taxes on your withdrawal as well as a penalty if you are under the age of 59 1/2.

Prior to joining any company, make sure that you fully understand the rules of any 401(k) plan that you may be eligible for. In particular, make sure that you know the company plan's rules pertaining to vesting and matching contributions. You can get this information from the plan's Summary Plan Description (SPD), which you can obtain from the Human Resources department at your new employer.

TRUTH

Borrowing from your 401(k)

Polonius, who in the play *Hamlet* advised his son to be neither a borrower nor a lender, would have been appalled at someone borrowing from his 401(k) account, because when you do so, you are, in fact, acting as both borrower and lender. But then again, Polonius didn't have to worry about mortgage payments on the castle or his horse breaking down.

Particularly when credit is tight, borrowing from yourself has a tremendous attraction. You don't have to go through a long and complicated application process or have your credit report scrutinized to be eligible for the loan. Qualifying and obtaining a loan from your 401(k) is both quick and easy. And perhaps best of all, you are borrowing the money from someone whom you totally trust: yourself.

The ability to borrow from your 401(k) account depends on the provisions of your particular plan. Although as many as 90% of plans do permit such borrowing, some do not, and others have limits and conditions to borrowing from your 401(k). A common limitation is that you may not borrow more than half of the balance of your 401(k) account with a $50,000 limit in any event. Some plans also limit the purposes of your loan to matters such as the purchase of a home, payment of education expenses, or medical costs. Most plans also require you to pay the money back to your 401(k) with interest within 15 years if you use the money to buy a home as well as require you to pay it back in as little as 5 years if you borrowed the money for any other purpose. The interest rate, which, in effect you are paying yourself, is commonly set at a point or two above the then in-effect prime rate.

> Borrowing from your own 401(k) account looks like an awfully good deal, but like many things that may appear to be awfully good at first, it may be just awful when you consider it more carefully.

The interest rate is an interesting matter when you are both borrower and lender. Generally, if you are lending money, you want a high interest rate, and if you are borrowing money, you want a low interest rate. In this instance, you are both borrower and lender.

All in all, borrowing from your own 401(k) account looks like an awfully good deal, but like many things that may appear to be awfully good at first, it may be just awful when you consider it more carefully.

Life is full of what–ifs, and the what-ifs when it comes to borrowing from your 401(k) can be pretty daunting. What if you don't repay your loan on time and you are under the age of 59 1/2? In that situation, not only are you subject to income tax on the amount of the loan, but you will also owe a penalty of 10% for what will be classified by the IRS as an early withdrawal.

Even if you do pay back the loan on time, in essence, you are subjecting yourself to being taxed twice on the same money: first when you repay the loan with after-tax dollars, and then when you eventually withdraw the money from your 401(k) account at retirement.

For many people, a better option is to borrow money through a home-equity loan, which not only provides a low interest rate for the loan, but allows you to deduct the interest you pay on your income taxes.

And what if you lose your job before you have paid back the loan? If you leave your job, either voluntarily or by being fired or laid off, you must generally repay your loan within 90 days or face a host of additional taxes and penalties.

Perhaps the worst element of a loan from your 401(k) is the best element of a 401(k)—namely, the tax-deferred compounding that occurs in your 401(k). When you borrow from your 401(k) account, you are reducing the amount of money that is in your 401(k) that would have been growing and compounding tax deferred. In fact, some plans even require you to pay back the loan before you can make any further contributions to your 401(k), so if you take out a loan from your 401(k) account, not only are you missing out on the tax-deferred compounding of the money you borrow from your 401(k), but also you are losing the opportunity to make more contributions to your 401(k) and having that money grow for you until you have completely paid back your loan.

In an effort to encourage younger workers to put more money into 401(k) accounts by providing greater access to their money through loans, a program titled the Reserve Solutions ReservePlus debit card enables employees to borrow from their 401(k) plans by establishing a credit line though their 401(k)s that they can draw upon through a debit card that they can use for purchases or even access by ATM withdrawals. The program seems simple and it is, but that simplicity can ultimately cost you money. When you set up the initial credit line, the entire amount of your credit line is removed from your other 401(k) investments and put into a money market fund. By doing this, you remove your money from higher-yielding investments such as index mutual funds and park the entire amount of your credit line in a low-yielding money market fund. So even if you are only borrowing $1,000 of a $20,000 credit line, the entire $20,000 credit line is growing at a greatly reduced rate. On top of that, the money market fund into which your money will be put carries higher fees than what you could find elsewhere. As I've said again and again, it isn't what you make that is important but what you keep. Higher expenses for any investment reduce your earnings, particularly over time.

For many people, a better option is to borrow money through a home-equity loan, which not only provides a low interest rate for the loan, but allows you to deduct the interest you pay on your income taxes. With a 401(k) loan, there is no tax deduction for the interest payment portion of your loan.

TRUTH

Company stock in 401(k)s

Many people are tempted to put the bulk of their 401(k) investments in their own company stock. Investment gurus are always telling people to invest in what they know, and who knows your own company better than you? Lower-level employees are constantly reading about higher-up company executives being rewarded with valuable stock options in the company. If the CEO believes strongly in the company, shouldn't the workers?

Perhaps the most common reason people invest largely in their own company's stock in their 401(k)s is that often a large portion of that money is free, where companies match with company stock the contributions of employees to their 401(k) accounts. According to a study by Hewitt Associates in 2006, company stock was the number-one choice of employees as an investment choice for their 401(k)s. It seems like a no-brainer to invest the bulk of your 401(k) account in company stock.

And, indeed, it is a no-brainer. Investing the bulk of your 401(k) investment in your company stock shows you have no brain or at least are not using what you have. All you have to do is think of one word: Enron. For those people who think that an Enron-like company destruction could never happen again, they should think again. It may, and it probably will. When Enron collapsed, employees lost as much as $850 million in their 401(k)s and stock option plans. Class action lawsuits against a slew of people, including managers of the 401(k) who were accused of not properly diversifying the plan funds, resulted in settlements that barely brought 25% of what was lost because people were blinded by greed, ignorance, and laziness.

> It doesn't make much sense to put all your eggs in one stock basket regardless of the company.

The wake of the fall of Enron has caused many companies and prudent employees to reconsider the position of company stock in 401(k)s. Profitable investment is about spreading your risk around so that if one segment of your investments does not do particularly well at that moment in time, your entire portfolio will still be in good shape because you have money in other types of investments. It doesn't make much sense to put all your eggs in one stock basket regardless of the company. The fact that you work for a particular company already means that you're invested in that company. To additionally put the lion's share of your 401(k) money into that same company's stock is just too risky.

The key to any successful investment portfolio, particularly for retirement investing, is diversification through asset allocation. Diversification through asset allocation involves dividing your investment among a variety of investment types, such as stocks, bonds, and money market funds. How much you allocate to each of these particular segments depends on your own tolerance for risk as well as your age. How comfortable are you taking a risk on investing the bulk of your money in stocks, which can provide the possibility of a greater return for your investment dollars but also carry the possibility of losing value and costing you money? Although tolerance for risk and age are not directly related, generally, the older you are, the less likely you are (or should be) to invest aggressively, because the risk of making a decision that works out badly is magnified when you don't have many years to make up for an unwise decision.

> **The key to any successful investment portfolio, particularly for retirement investing, is diversification through asset allocation.**

A number of formulas are used to determine the optimum division of stocks and bonds in a retirement investment portfolio. One formula determines the amount of bonds in your portfolio by multiplying your age by 80%, with the remainder of your portfolio to be held in stock or mutual funds. For example, using this formula, a 65-year-old woman should invest 52% of her assets in bonds and 48% in stock mutual funds.

Using a variety of low-cost index mutual funds to form the basis of the stock portion of your 401(k) is a simple strategy that not only has proven to be effective in the long run but also increases your profit because the fees of index mutual funds are considerably less than many other choices available to you in your 401(k). For those people uncomfortable making the decision as to how to divide their investments between stocks and bonds within their 401(k), many plans have begun to provide more target fund options that adjust the balance between your stocks and bonds according to formulas based on your age and the time remaining until your retirement.

Fortunately, some companies have learned the lessons of Enron either out of a desire to best benefit their employees and help them plan for retirement or out of blatant self-preservation and fear of lawsuits by disgruntled employees. Reading the handwriting on the courtroom walls, many companies have chosen to stop making their matching contributions to employees' 401(k) accounts in the form of company stock.

If you work for a company that had or still does provide company stock to match your contribution to your 401(k) account, it does not make sense to give up that free money. However, most experts believe that the value of your company stock should not exceed 10% of the value of your 401(k). If you find that your company stock represents a greater percentage than that, you may wish to consider selling some of that stock to bring your 401(k) portfolio more in line with a properly diversified asset allocation. Federal law passed in the wake of the Enron debacle permits you to sell any shares that your employer used to match your 401(k) contribution after you have been with the company for three years.

The bottom line is that there's nothing wrong with having your company stock in your 401(k), but just as no single stock should dominate your portfolio outside your 401(k), so should no single stock dominate your portfolio inside your 401(k).

TRUTH

31

IRAs, 401(k)s, and creditors

The simple answer to whether your 401(k) is subject to the claims of your creditors, such as a credit card company, is that it is not. Federal law exempts your 401(k) from the claims of almost anyone who has a claim against you. Of course, there are exceptions to every rule, and even 401(k)s may be subject to claims in a divorce or for child support. As for the federal government, its guiding rule is the Golden Rule; however, its version of the Golden Rule is that because the federal government has the gold, it makes the rules, and its rules generally allow the IRS and other federal agencies to get at your 401(k) despite the general rule that 401(k) accounts are not subject to the claims of creditors.

However, when it comes to IRAs, the simple answer is that there is no simple answer as to whether your IRA is subject to the claims of creditors. The changes in the bankruptcy laws that went into effect in 2005 not only protect 401(k)s from the claims of creditors in a bankruptcy, but also protect IRAs from the claims of your creditors in a bankruptcy. On the surface, this might make you feel safe as to the protection that the law provides for your IRA from your creditors. However, a closer reading of the law indicates that you get this federal protection of your IRA against the claims of your creditors only if you are in bankruptcy. So unless you actually file a bankruptcy, your IRA is not protected by federal law from your creditors. Instead, state law controls whether your IRA is protected from your creditors.

There is great variance in the amount of protection provided by the individual states. Some states also give differing protection to traditional IRAs and Roth IRAs. Certain states limit protection of IRAs to the amount in the IRA that is reasonably necessary for the IRA owner's support. In practice, this may be limited to around $100,000 although it certainly can vary. Finally, as with 401(k)s, IRAs may be subject to claims in a divorce or for child support. With that being said, here is a list of the states and the protection they provide to your IRA from the claims of your creditors:

> The simple answer to whether your 401(k) is subject to the claims of your creditors, such as a credit card company, is that it is not.

Alabama	Protects traditional IRAs, but not Roth IRAs
Alaska	Protects all IRAs
Arizona	Protects all IRAs
Arkansas	Protects IRAs only up to $20,000
California	Protects IRAs up to the extent reasonably necessary for support
Colorado	Protects all IRAs
Connecticut	Protects all IRAs
Delaware	Protects all IRAs
Florida	Protects all IRAs
Georgia	Protects traditional IRAs up to the extent reasonably necessary for support, but does not protect Roth IRAs
Hawaii	Protects all IRA funds that have been deposited more than three years
Idaho	Protects all IRAs
Illinois	Protects all IRAs
Indiana	Protects all IRAs
Iowa	Protects all IRAs
Kansas	Protects all IRAs
Kentucky	Protects all IRAs
Louisiana	Protects all IRA funds that have been deposited more than one year
Maine	Protects all IRA funds up to the extent reasonably necessary for support
Maryland	Protects all IRAs
Massachusetts	Protects all IRAs subject to excess contributions in previous five years

Michigan	Protects all IRAs
Minnesota	Protects IRAs up to $60,000, which is indexed for inflation
Mississippi	Protects all IRAs
Missouri	Protects all IRA funds up to the extent reasonably necessary for support
Montana	Protects all IRA funds
Nebraska	Protects all IRA funds up to the extent reasonably necessary for support
Nevada	Protects all IRA funds up to $500,000
New Hampshire	Protects all IRA funds
New Jersey	Protects all IRA funds
New Mexico	Protects all IRA funds
New York	Protects all IRA funds
North Carolina	Protects all IRA funds
North Dakota	Protects IRA funds up to $200,000 or more if needed for reasonably necessary support
Ohio	Protects all IRA funds up to the extent reasonably necessary for support
Oklahoma	Protects all IRA funds
Oregon	Protects all IRA funds
Pennsylvania	Protects all IRA funds other than those contributed within previous year
Rhode Island	Does not protect IRA funds
South Carolina	Protects all IRA funds up to the extent reasonably necessary for support
South Dakota	Protects IRA funds up to $250,000

Tennessee	Protects all IRA funds
Texas	Protects all IRA funds
Utah	Protects all IRA funds other than those contributed within previous year
Vermont	Protects all IRA funds other than those contributed to self-directed IRAs within the previous year
Virginia	Protects IRA funds up to an amount to produce an annual distribution of $25,000 per year
Washington	Protects all IRA funds
West Virginia	Protects all IRA funds and distributions to the extent reasonably necessary for support
Wisconsin	Protects all IRA funds up to the extent reasonably necessary for support
Wyoming	Does not protect IRAs

Now, if this just didn't seem complicated enough, remember that the determination of the law to be applied in determining whether your IRA will be protected from your creditors may depend on either where you live or where the IRA is held, which may be in another state. Once again, the law is not a model of clarity as to which will apply. The best course of action is to seek legal guidance in the state where you live.

TRUTH

32

Automatic 401(k) enrollment

Many of us tend to follow Mark Twain's advice of never putting off until tomorrow what we can put off until the day after tomorrow. The consequences of procrastinating minor things, such as delaying getting an oil change for your car an extra 1,000 miles, may not be particularly serious, but when it comes to retirement planning, putting off a decision to start saving can seriously damage your retirement plans.

The key to successful investing is time. It may seem obvious, but the longer your money is invested, the more you're going to earn. And even when (not if) the inevitable downturns in the stock market occur, if you have been invested for the long haul, you are in a better position to weather these momentary market declines, because your money has been there working for you during the good years and will be ready to capitalize on the opportunities that will be there when the market starts heading upward again. The secret to long-term investing is compound interest.

The concept of compound interest is actually quite simple. When you invest and earn interest on your investment in one year, the next year you are earning interest not just on your initial investment but also on the interest that you earned in the previous year. A corollary of the theory of compound interest is the rule of 72. According to this rule, you can determine the time it will take to double your investment by dividing the number 72 by the interest rate. For example, if you were earning 5% interest on your investment, it would double in value in 14.4 years. Of course, if you were earning more than 5%, your money would grow even faster. The average annual rate of return on investments in the stock market is 10%. Of course, there are years that you will earn less than that, but there will also be years that you will earn considerably more than that.

For many employees, automatic enrollment in their company's 401(k) plan may be the best decision they never make.

When you invest in a 401(k), you not only get compound interest working for you, but you also have tax deferral working for you as well. With a traditional 401(k), you are not taxed on the amount of your salary that you contribute to your 401(k), so some of your contribution that would have been lost to income taxes is instead now working hard for you in your 401(k). You do not have to pay income taxes on this money until you take it out of your 401(k) at retirement years later, thereby enabling more of your money to compound and work for you. With a traditional 401(k), you pay less income tax than you would otherwise, while more of your money grows undisturbed by the tentacles of the IRS. Sounds pretty good, eh? It is.

So why doesn't everyone who has the opportunity to invest in a 401(k) at work do so? There are a lot of reasons why people don't act. Some people are fearful of making a financial mistake. Some people don't understand the benefits of 401(k)s. And some are just plain lazy.

> Under the new automatic enrollment rules, employers can pick a default investment choice if the employee fails to make a choice.

That is where automatic enrollment in 401(k)s come in. The Pension Protection Act of 2006 simplified auto-enrollment in a 401(k). Before this legislation was enacted, most people had the option of enrolling in a company's 401(k) plan when they joined the company, but for the usual reasons, some people just didn't take advantage of this tremendous retirement saving opportunity. In these employees' case, their failure to make a decision was tantamount to making a decision to not save for retirement. Now if you do nothing, you are automatically enrolled in your company's 401(k) plan when you're hired.

Of course, you have to make some decisions when you enroll in a 401(k) plan, such as how much you want to contribute and where you want your contributions invested. Too many people have invested all of their 401(k) contributions in conservative money market funds. There's nothing wrong with money market funds. They have a place in everyone's portfolio of investments. But the fact is that money market funds are just too conservative to achieve the kind of growth that you need over time to achieve a successful retirement. Under the new automatic enrollment rules, employers can pick a default investment choice if the employee fails to make a choice. Many companies are now choosing target mutual funds that provide a mixture of stocks and bonds geared toward a particular target date of retirement. The balance between stocks and bonds is adjusted by the mutual fund each year to attain the optimum mixture of safety and profit. The use of a target fund provides a much greater opportunity for growth than merely parking your money in a money market fund.

Under the new 401(k) automatic enrollment rules, employers are permitted to set the automatic contribution levels for new employees at a level of at least 3% of the employee's compensation. The law also provides for an automatic escalation of the contribution amount by a percentage point each year, up to a minimum 6% contribution amount by the fourth year of contributions. Companies that do this must contribute matching funds at a level of at least 2% and as much as 3%. They also must provide full vesting for employees within two years of participation.

All of this sounds pretty good, but what if you really don't want to take advantage of your company's plan? In that event, the law permits you to opt out of the automatic enrollment without penalties or taxes within 90 days.

Many companies are taking the automatic enrollment a step further and contacting their current employees who are not enrolled in the company 401(k) plan. They give them a notice allowing them to be automatically enrolled by merely checking a box that allows them to join the company 401(k) plan with the same default options as are given to new employees.

For many employees, automatic enrollment in their company's 401(k) plan may be the best decision they never make.

TRUTH

33

Roth 401(k)s

The popularity of the Roth IRA, where you can save for retirement in an account that grows totally tax free, has spawned the latest development in retirement planning, the Roth 401(k). Many people are familiar with conventional 401(k) retirement accounts where an employee is able to contribute some of his salary into a tax-deferred retirement account. Money contributed to a conventional 401(k) account is not subject to income tax at the time that it is invested into the 401(k) account. However, income taxes become due when the money is withdrawn from the account.

Starting in 2006, employers could offer Roth 401(k) accounts that permit employees to put all or some of their 401(k) contributions into a Roth 401(k) account. The amount of the worker's salary that is contributed into the Roth 401(k) is part of the taxable wages for the worker in the year that the money is contributed to the Roth 401(k). However, once the money is deposited into the Roth 401(k) account, it grows tax free and may be withdrawn later without incurring income taxes. I'll let you in on a little secret: The Roth 401(k) really shouldn't even be called a 401(k) because the law authorizing it is actually Internal Revenue Code Section 402A, but why quibble?

Similar to a regular 401(k) account, an employee could contribute as much as $15,500 in 2008 to his Roth 401(k) account if he were younger than age 50. Employees over 50 may contribute an additional $5,000, for a maximum contribution of as much as $20,500. Although these are the amounts that federal law permits as a maximum contribution, employers may set a lesser limit for their own particular plans, such as a limit of an employee's contribution to a maximum of 10% of his salary, which in the case of a person earning $75,000 would be $7,500.

Loophole

Although in 2008 a person could not fully qualify to contribute the maximum $5,000 for a Roth IRA unless his annual income was less than $101,000 for a single person and less than $159,000 if he were married, there are no income eligibility requirements to qualify for a Roth 401(k). Therefore, higher earners who would otherwise be unable to take advantage of the considerable tax savings of a Roth IRA can get those same advantages through a Roth 401(k).

An employee whose employer offers both types of 401(k) accounts has the option of taking advantage of both types of retirement accounts so long as the total money contributed to the regular 401(k) and the Roth 401(k) does not exceed the total amount that he can contribute under the terms of the plan. For example, a worker over the age of 50 who is eligible under federal law and the terms of the particular plan at his place of work to contribute $15,500 could choose to put half of that contribution or $7,750 in a regular 401(k) and another $7,750 in a Roth 401(k).

Higher earners who would otherwise be unable to take advantage of the considerable tax savings of a Roth IRA can get those same advantages through a Roth 401(k).

Glass half empty

Sorry to bring you some bad news, but although employers are permitted under federal law and many do choose to provide some amount of matching funds to the contributions of their workers to traditional 401(k) accounts, thereby giving free money to the retirement accounts of participating workers, no such matching contributions may be made by employers into the Roth 401(k) accounts of employees. However, the glass really is half full, because the employer may make a matching contribution into a regular 401(k) account on behalf of the employee when the employee has contributed to a Roth 401(k) with the company.

Choices

So which choice is better: the regular or the Roth 401(k)? Younger workers who are not likely to retire for many years might find the advantages of years and years of the tax-free growth of a Roth 401(k) account to be of more value than the mere deferring of income taxes until retirement. In addition, lower-paid workers may find that the present tax deferral is not worth as much to them as totally tax-free growth. Employees who are not eligible for a Roth IRA because their incomes are too high may find the opportunity to take advantage of tax-free growth in a Roth 401(k) more tempting. Those workers who are convinced that income tax rates are likely to go up in the future may be more inclined to take the tax-free growth provided by a Roth 401(k) rather than the tax deferral offered by the regular 401(k).

Fortunately, you really can't make a bad choice. Deciding between a regular 401(k) account and a Roth 401(k) account is a decision where you can't lose regardless of which type of 401(k) you choose. In addition, for those people who qualify for a Roth IRA, they can not only continue to contribute to their Roth IRA, but also contribute to a Roth 401(k) at work in the same year, thus enabling them to put away as much as $26,000 in 2008 if they are over the age of 50.

Until recently, many companies did not offer Roth 401(k) accounts. Many companies were concerned that the law that authorized these accounts was set to sunset on December 31, 2010, and that setting up such accounts for only the few years since they were authorized in 2006 until 2011 was not worth the cost of doing so. However, with the passage of the Pension Protection Act of 2006, the law permitting Roth 401(k) accounts has been made permanent. Consequently, more and more companies are now offering Roth 401(k)s, including such large companies as IBM, General Motors, and Johnson & Johnson.

Picky little detail

Unlike with a Roth IRA, an employee with a Roth 401(k) is required to start taking minimum distributions from the account upon reaching the age of 70. On the plus side, those minimum distributions will still be tax free. On the negative side, those amounts taken as minimum distributions will reduce the amount of tax-free growth of the account.

Loophole to the rescue

You can avoid the minimum distribution problem altogether by rolling over the Roth 401(k) at retirement into a Roth IRA, which has no such requirement for required minimum distributions. Now aren't you glad you bought this book?

34

Traditional IRA, Roth IRA, 401(k), or Roth 401(k)

We all know that we should be saving as much as we can for retirement. Traditional IRAs, Roth IRAs, 401(k)s, and Roth 401(k)s all have distinct advantages as well as some disadvantages. Some people even think that if they have enough money to do so, they should hedge their bets and put money into all four types of retirement savings vehicles available to them.

But if you had to make a choice, what should it be?

Traditional IRA vs. Roth IRA

Much of the benefit of the Roth IRA as compared to the traditional IRA is that when you take money out of your Roth IRA at retirement, you are not required to pay income taxes on that money. If tax rates increase, which is certainly a distinct possibility, the Roth IRA is the better choice. However, if you believe you will be in a lower tax bracket at retirement than you are now, you may find that you are better off, if you are able to make deductible contributions to your traditional IRA, by contributing to a traditional IRA, reducing your present and very real tax burden and having more money work for you, compounding tax deferred. If you are not eligible for a deductible traditional IRA, the decision is an easy one. If you are eligible for a Roth IRA, you will be better off with it than contributing to a traditional nondeductible IRA.

You also may wish to consider the enhanced flexibility of a Roth IRA, which does not require you to take mandatory distributions at 70 1/2 as is required with a traditional IRA. In addition, with a Roth IRA, you always have access to the money you put into the Roth IRA without penalty at any time, whereas there are substantial penalties if you withdraw money from a traditional IRA before you reach the age of 59 1/2 with some specific, but quite limited exceptions.

Also, in your early earning years, you may be in a lower tax bracket, and it may make more sense to put your money into a Roth IRA. As your income and your income taxes go up, you may wish to get the present tax relief of adding a traditional IRA to your mix of retirement vehicles as your age and your income increase.

401(k) vs. Roth IRA

If the choice is to put money into either a traditional 401(k) or a Roth 401(k) at work or contribute to a Roth IRA on your own, you will find that the fees you incur in either type of 401(k) plan at work will most likely be significantly higher than you will incur in a Roth IRA. And as everyone should be aware, the money that you lose to excessive or unnecessary fees can seriously reduce the amount of your money that is actually working for you in your retirement accounts. You will also have many more investment choices in your own Roth IRA as compared to either type of 401(k). This means that you can choose the retirement investments that are best suited to you and your tolerance for risk. Finally, you may want to consider that the money invested in stock mutual funds in a traditional 401(k) will not only be taxed when withdrawn at retirement but will also be taxed at higher ordinary income tax rates rather than lower capital gains rates that would apply if the investor held those same stock mutual funds privately outside of a traditional 401(k). With a Roth IRA, the question of income taxes is moot. There aren't any. However, the one advantage that a 401(k) has that a Roth IRA does not have is that no one is going to be making matching

> You have many more investment choices in your own Roth IRA as compared to either type of 401(k).

contributions into your Roth IRA, while your employer may be making matching contributions to your 401(k). That's free money, and that's good.

Traditional 401(k) vs. Roth 401(k)

Younger workers who are not high wage earners might be more inclined to take advantage of the tax-free growth of a Roth 401(k) rather than merely defer income taxes, particularly when their lower tax bracket might minimize the value of the deduction. On the other end of the spectrum, employees who are not eligible for a Roth IRA due to their incomes being too high may find attractive the opportunity to take advantage of the tax-free growth that the Roth 401(k) provides. It is important to note that, despite the fact that a Roth 401(k) is not eligible for matching contributions by employers, an employee may have both a Roth 401(k) and a traditional 401(k) into which his employer's matching contribution may be made.

Another option

Another option, if you qualify, is to maintain your contributions to your company's traditional 401(k) plan sufficient to obtain any company matching contributions and then own a separate Roth IRA that you contribute the maximum amount to. This strategy hedges your bet in regard to possible future tax increases while maximizing the money that you have working for you in your company's 401(k).

The first step

Before you start contributing to a retirement plan, you may wish to look at your debt. Although your mortgage interest is deductible, there are no corresponding tax benefits to most other debt. If, like many people, you carry substantial credit card balances at interest rates that often appear to be constantly increasing, you would be better served by paying off that credit card debt before you do any retirement planning. You will get more bang for your buck. The exception to this rule is that, if your company's traditional 401(k) plan offers matching contributions by your employer, you would be wise to contribute to your company's traditional 401(k) as much as is necessary to achieve the maximum employer matching contributions. Don't say no to free money that can be working for you. However, once you've met the requirements for matching funds in your company's traditional 401(k), pay off that credit card debt as soon as possible.

TRUTH

35

401(k) choices when you leave your job

People leave their jobs for any number of reasons, from needing to relocate to finding a higher paying position. But what happens to your 401(k) when you leave your job? As so often is the case, there is more than one option, with some options much better than others when it comes to your financial well-being.

The easiest decision to make is to merely not make a decision, which, by default, becomes your decision. By not making any provisions for your 401(k) when you leave your present employment, you have made the choice to leave your 401(k) account with your now former employer's plan. This is not necessarily a bad decision, but it does expose you to unnecessary additional management fees, particularly if it results in your having multiple 401(k) accounts with multiple present and past employers. As always, money lost to fees is money that is not growing and compounding for you.

Cashing in your 401(k) account when you leave a job potentially turns you into a double loser.

Your second option is to roll your 401(k) account from your previous employer's plan into the plan at your new place of employment. Before you make this decision, you should carefully evaluate both the choices of investments available to you in your new employer's 401(k) plan as well as the administrative costs that you will incur by being enrolled in your new employer's 401(k) plan. You may find that you are actually better off by exercising your third option, which is to roll the money from your previous employer's 401(k) plan into a self-directed IRA. By choosing this option, you put yourself in a better position to not only choose the investments that form the basis of your retirement account, but also have more control over the fees that will be incurred.

Warning

Read the fine print in your 401(k) plan carefully when comparing the fees you pay within the account to fees you would pay if you rolled the account into a self-directed IRA. Sometimes what may appear to be lower fees in your former company's 401(k) plan are limited to current employees of the company. Some plans mandate higher fees for participants in the company 401(k) plan who are no longer employed by the company.

Regardless of whether you roll over your 401(k) funds from your previous employer into your new employer's plan or into your own self-directed IRA, you will still be able to continue the tax deferral that your 401(k) provided. If your former 401(k) was a Roth 401(k), you can continue the tax-free compounding provided in the Roth 401(k) by rolling it into another Roth 401(k) or a self-directed Roth IRA.

Some people choose to either leave their money in their former employer's 401(k) plan or move it into their new employer's 401(k) plan so that in the future they have the option of borrowing money from it. This option is not available with an IRA. However, in general, borrowing from a 401(k) account is not a good idea. It is true that by borrowing from yourself, you are paying yourself the interest on a loan that you would otherwise be paying someone else. However, by reducing the balance of your 401(k) account through borrowing from it, you are drastically reducing the value of the tax-deferred compounding of the funds in your 401(k) account, which is the main reason for having one. Further, if you leave your job, either voluntarily or involuntarily, you are required to pay back the loan with interest within 60 days. If you fail to make this required repayment in a timely fashion, you will be subject to income taxes on the loan amount and a 10% early withdrawal penalty if you are not over the age of 59 1/2. All in all, borrowing from your 401(k) is not a sound proposition.

Prior to the enactment of the Pension Protection Act of 2006, there was an incentive for workers to take money out of their former 401(k) plan when they left their jobs so they could take advantage of laws that permitted stretch IRAs, which provide for the continuation of tax-deferral benefits for many years for people inheriting the IRA. Now, however, these benefits are available to people inheriting 401(k) accounts, so the necessity to move funds out of a 401(k) account to take advantage of stretch IRA provisions are no longer a factor in the choice as to what to do with 401(k) funds when leaving a job.

For people who live by the motto "Buy me, gimme, take me, get me," the temptation to take the money from a 401(k) account and spend it when leaving a job is tremendous. This, however, is one instance where you should avoid the advice of Oscar Wilde, who said, "The only way to get rid of temptation is to yield to it." Cashing in your 401(k) account when you leave a job potentially turns you into a double loser. You not only lose by paying income tax on all the money you withdraw, but you also have to pay an additional 10% penalty for an early withdrawal from your 401(k) if you are under the age of 59 1/2. Not to mention the fact (which I now mention) that you lose out on continuing tax-deferred growth of the funds withdrawn. Unfortunately, according to a Hewitt Associates study done in 2005, 45% of workers do cash in their 401(k) accounts when they leave a job.

Loophole

A little-known provision of the Internal Revenue Code permits former employees who had their company's stock in their 401(k) accounts to transfer that stock into a regular investment account. This is considered an *in-kind distribution* that subjects the former employee to income taxes only on the value of the company stock at the time she bought it. This means, for example, that if the stock was worth $5,000 at the time the former employee initially purchased it for her 401(k) account and the stock is now worth $50,000, the former employee would only pay income taxes on $5,000 when she takes the money out of the company 401(k) plan. The remainder of the stock value is permitted to continue to grow. When the former employee ultimately sells the stock, income taxes will be assessed at lower capital gains rates.

TRUTH

36

401(k) transfers

Pass it on. When you have something good, it is only natural to want to pass it on to the ones you love. Passing on a 401(k) with its tax-deferral qualities still intact is a gift that can keep on giving, as the people you transfer it to can continue to defer taxes over the rest of their lives.

The ability to transfer an IRA at death to a spouse or even a nonspouse has been established for some time, but the ability to transfer a 401(k) account at death to an inherited IRA for a nonspouse beneficiary has only been allowed since the enactment of the Pension Protection Act of 2006. Previously, if an employee remained active in his company's 401(k) plan rather than transferring his 401(k) into an IRA, at his death, the money had to be distributed to the designated beneficiary of the 401(k), but without the ability to extend the tax deferral provided by the 401(k).

However, according to the IRS's interpretation of the Pension Protection Act of 2006, the ability of nonspouses to stretch their withdrawals from inherited 401(k) accounts over their lifetimes was not made a mandatory requirement of all 401(k) plans but was merely an option available to companies. Congress had intended for this provision of the law to be mandatory for all companies. Despite initial optimism that the IRS would accede to the wishes of Congress, the IRS continues to interpret the law as saying that it is optional for companies to include a provision for nonspouses to be able to stretch their inherited 401(k) withdrawals. The bottom line is that you should make sure you understand the specific provisions of your company's plan.

> The IRS continues to interpret the law as saying that it is optional for companies to include a provision for nonspouses to be able to stretch their inherited 401(k) withdrawals.

As always, there are many rules, some obscure and all critical that must be met to accomplish the desired result of passing on a 401(k) in a manner to permit the continuation of tax deferral over the lifetime of the new beneficiary of the account.

First and foremost, the transfer must be done by the end of the calendar year following the year in which the employee who owned the 401(k) account died. The transfer itself must be trustee-to-trustee, which means that the surviving beneficiary of the account may not receive the funds directly. Rather, the trustee of the 401(k) account must transfer the funds in the account directly to the custodian of the inherited IRA on behalf of the beneficiary. In the case of the beneficiary being a surviving spouse, the funds may be transferred to the spouse's own IRA.

As we learned in the movie *A League of Their Own*, there's no crying in baseball. There also are no mulligans (do-overs) in 401(k) transfers. If inherited 401(k) funds are distributed directly to a spouse or nonspouse who intends to put the funds into, in the case of a surviving spouse, his own IRA or, in the case of an inheriting nonspouse, an inherited IRA, there will be tears, no second chance to correct the situation, increased taxes, and lost opportunity. In this event, the entire amount of the 401(k) account becomes immediately taxable, and the opportunity to continue tax deferral over the lifetime of the beneficiary is lost forever.

When a nonspouse inherits a 401(k) account, the title of the IRA that the 401(k) account is transferred into is very important, because if it is not titled correctly, there will be significant tax penalties. Although a surviving spouse as beneficiary of a 401(k) account can merely have the account rolled over into his own existing IRA account, a nonspouse beneficiary must have the funds transferred into a new IRA that is designated an inherited IRA. An example of a properly titled inherited IRA is "Homer Simpson deceased, inherited IRA for the benefit of Lisa Simpson."

Always critical are the rules regarding Required Minimum Distributions, and inherited 401(k) accounts are no exception. Regardless of the age of the person receiving the inherited 401(k) account, he must start taking his Required Minimum Distribution from the inherited IRA by December 31 of the year immediately following the year of the death of the holder of the 401(k) account.

Strict attention should also be paid to whether the deceased 401(k) holder had started receiving his own required minimum distributions prior to death. If the 401(k) account holder was under the age of 70 1/2 and had not reached his required beginning date, no distributions from the 401(k) account must be made before transferring the 401(k) account to the IRA of a surviving spouse beneficiary or the inherited IRA of a nonspouse beneficiary. However, if the 401(k) account holder dies on or after his required beginning date, a required distribution is necessary for the year of his death. If the 401(k) account holder had already taken the required distribution for that year before his death, nothing further must be done; however, if the distribution was not done prior to death, that minimum required distribution amount for the deceased 401(k) account holder must be taken directly by the beneficiary and must not be included in the amount of the account rolled over into either the spouse's own IRA or the nonspouse beneficiary's inherited IRA.

A trust can be the beneficiary of a transferred 401(k) account. The requirements for a trust being a beneficiary of an IRA receiving funds from a transferred 401(k) are discussed in Truth 10, "Trusts as IRA Beneficiaries." So long as these requirements are met, the trust can serve as a valid beneficiary of a 401(k) account rolled into an inherited IRA.

TRUTH
37

Individual 401(k)

The newest choice in the arsenal of tax-advantaged retirement investment programs is the Individual 401(k), sometimes known as the Solo 401(k), named after its sponsor Napoleon Solo, the hero of the '60s television show, *The Man from U.N.C.L.E.* All right, it isn't really named after Napoleon Solo, but it should have been. The Individual 401(k) was a product of the Economic Growth and Tax Relief Reconciliation Act of 2001 that goes by the imposing and difficult-to-pronounce acronym, EGTRRA.

An Individual 401(k) is a terrific retirement tool that is limited to self-employed people who are running businesses with no employees other than themselves or their spouses. Partners are also permitted to use the Individual 401(k) when, other than the partners and their wives, no one else works for the partnership.

Perhaps the major benefit of an Individual 401(k) is that it permits the contribution of more of a person's income to a tax-deferred retirement investment plan than could be done through an IRA. An Individual 401(k) contribution has two components. The first, in 2008, is the lesser of your total compensation, or $15,500. The second component, which is related to profit sharing, is limited to 25% of the employee's compensation if the business is incorporated or 20% of the employee's self-employment income if the business is a sole proprietorship or a partnership. In any event, the total amount that can be contributed is $45,000 in 2008. This figure will rise with inflation in future years. In addition, the law permits an additional catch-up contribution for people who are at least 50, for a total annual contribution of $50,000.

An advantage of the Individual 401(k) is that if your business is not particularly profitable in any one year, you can choose whether to contribute at all or at whatever level you want to your Individual 401(k).

As with a traditional 401(k), the money you contribute to your

> An Individual 401(k) is a terrific retirement tool that is limited to self-employed people who are running businesses with no employees other than themselves or their spouses.

Individual 401(k) grows tax deferred until you take the money out. The same rules for early withdrawals for traditional 401(k)s also apply to Individual 401(k)s.

Opportunity knocking

Because the first $15,500 that you contributes to your Individual 401(k) is not limited to a percentage of your compensation, you, most likely, will be able to contribute much more money to an Individual 401(k) than you could to a SEP IRA, where there are such limitations. This is particularly helpful if you have a side business that you don't earn a lot of money from but wish to take the opportunity to shelter as much as possible from taxes to grow toward your future retirement. For example, if you have a regular job but also have a side business that you've earned $15,500 from, you can put the entire amount of your income from the side business into an Individual 401(k).

However, note that if you have a regular 401(k) at a job, the amount that you can contribute to your Individual 401(k) is reduced by the amount of any contributions that you made to your regular 401(k) at your primary job. Fortunately, though, this limitation does not affect the 20% or 25% of your business income that you are allowed to contribute to your Individual 401(k).

Picky little detail

Even though you don't have to actually put the money into your Individual 401(k) before the April 15 filing date for your income tax return, you must establish the plan by December 31 of the previous year to take advantage of the Individual 401(k) for that previous year.

As with other 401(k)s, a benefit (or temptation, if you wish to describe it in that fashion) of an Individual 401(k) is the ability to borrow from your 401(k). You can borrow up to half of the value of your Individual 401(k), up to a maximum of $50,000. Usually you must pay back these loans within five years, although if the loan is used to help finance the purchase of your home, the loan's repayment can be extended to as long as 15 years. As with other traditional 401(k) loans, there are stiff penalties for the failure to repay the loan in a timely fashion.

The loan feature may be particularly attractive to an entrepreneurial self-employed individual who may wish to borrow money from her own retirement fund to help the business when needed rather than face the sometimes difficult process of qualifying for a business loan from a bank.

Fees

Fees and costs are a concern to everyone, but particularly to self-employed businesspeople trying to squeeze as much value as possible out of every dollar expended. An Individual 401(k) plan is easy to set up and easy to administer, which translates into less cost, although these costs may not be as low as those involved with a SEP IRA.

Consolidation

The law also provides you with more flexibility by allowing you to consolidate traditional IRAs, SEP IRAs, SIMPLE IRAs, and other retirement plans into your Individual 401(k). This feature is particularly helpful to a self-employed person who may wish to both lower the costs of administering a number of different retirement accounts as well as take retirement accounts that would not permit loans and put them into the 401(k), which does.

All in all, an Individual 401(k) provides self-employed people with an opportunity to put away more money for retirement than a SEP IRA while providing a source of funds that they can borrow from if they need it, which a SEP IRA does not allow. The costs may be marginally higher to maintain an Individual 401(k) than a SEP IRA, but many people believe that they are well worth it.

TRUTH

38

SIMPLE 401(k)

For small business owners who see the virtue and cost savings of simplicity, a SIMPLE 401(k) may be just what, if not the doctor, the accountant ordered. As with the SIMPLE IRA, the boldly lettered SIMPLE is not just descriptive of this type of retirement plan but also is an acronym for Savings Incentive Match Plan for Employees. Just as an aside, I think it would be a great job to be in charge of coming up with the acronyms for federal programs.

The SIMPLE 401(k) takes elements of the SIMPLE IRA and blends them with elements of a traditional 401(k) to come up with a simpler (no surprise), less costly version of a 401(k) plan. Similar to the SIMPLE IRA, the SIMPLE 401(k) is limited to companies that have no more than 100 employees. Employees can contribute a percentage of their salary through a salary reduction contribution that is limited in 2008 to $10,500. This is less than the $15,500 that may be contributed to a traditional 401(k). After 2008, this amount will be adjusted annually for inflation. In addition, as with the SIMPLE IRA, if the particular company plan permits it, an additional catch-up contribution of $2,500 by employees who are at least 50 years of age is authorized by law. This amount is less than the catch-up provision in a traditional 401(k), which in 2008 is $5,000, which is double the amount of the permitted catch-up provision in a SIMPLE 401(k).

If your employer offers a SIMPLE 401(k), don't assume that you will have all the features of a traditional 401(k).

As with traditional 401(k) plans, the employer may choose to match the contribution of the employee. Matching contributions are determined by the individual employers but are limited to no more than 3% of the employee's compensation. Alternatively, an employer may choose instead of making matching contributions to contribute to individual employees' SIMPLE 401(k) accounts 2% of the compensation of employees earning at least $5,000 per year who have been with the company for at least one year although, like the SIMPLE IRA, the one year of employment requirement for eligibility to participate in the company SIMPLE 401(k) plan may be waived by the company in its own particular plan.

Unlike matching contributions to a traditional 401(k), employers who use a SIMPLE 401(k) may not delay the vesting of full rights to employer contributions. Employees have an immediate right to everything contributed to their SIMPLE 401(k) account.

Unlike the SIMPLE IRA, federal law permits the SIMPLE 401(k), like the traditional 401(k), to allow participants to borrow money from their own 401(k) account, although it is up to the individual employers sponsoring their company plans as to whether this particular provision will be included in the company's plan. This is often a costly provision for an employer to include, particularly the small employer who is most likely to use the SIMPLE 401(k). However, it is a plan provision that many employees find attractive. They have a ready source of money to borrow from, and by borrowing from themselves, the money they pay in interest ultimately goes to their benefit. Others, though, find this less of an attractive feature and more of a temptation.

Although the law permits the loans to be used for any reason, including a trip to Las Vegas, individual employers are allowed to limit the use of borrowed money from a SIMPLE 401(k) to purposes such as educational expenses, prevention of eviction of the employee from his home, unreimbursed medical costs, or for a first-time home purchase.

Generally, the loan programs within a SIMPLE 401(k) permit you to borrow as much as half of your balance, to a maximum of $50,000. The usual length of time of the loan is five years, and the interest rate is attractive, commonly prime plus one or two percentage points. However, unlike money that you borrow from a home equity loan, the interest that you pay yourself through a loan from your SIMPLE 401(k) is not tax deductible.

There are a couple of other major concerns regarding SIMPLE 401(k) loans. First, if you leave your job for any reason, you're required to pay back the loan, usually within 60 days, or be subject to both taxes and penalties. Second, the money that you have borrowed from your SIMPLE 401(k) is no longer sheltered within your SIMPLE 401(k) and growing and compounding on a tax-deferred basis, which is why you put the money there in the first place.

Another attractive feature of the SIMPLE 401(k) as compared to the SIMPLE IRA is the possibility of being able to take a hardship withdrawal as you can from a traditional 401(k). Again, all plans are not required by law to offer this provision, but employers may choose to do so. Unlike a loan from your SIMPLE 401(k), the money that you take out of your SIMPLE 401(k) through a hardship withdrawal need not be paid back. The law limits the use of such funds to specific purposes such as these:

■ Paying for unreimbursed medical expenses for yourself or your family

■ Buying yourself a home

■ Paying higher education costs for yourself or family members

■ Paying rent or mortgage amounts necessary to avoid eviction or foreclosure

Before you get too excited, note that if you do take a hardship withdrawal from your SIMPLE 401(k) and you are under the age of 59 1/2, you will be subject to income taxes on the amount you withdraw as well as a 10% early withdrawal penalty. If you are in the 28% tax bracket and under the age of 59 1/2, taking an early withdrawal can eat up as much as 35% to 45% of the money you withdraw. There are some exceptions to this harsh treatment, but they are quite limited, such as when you are totally disabled.

The bottom line is that all the bells and whistles of a SIMPLE 401(k) come at a price to the employer providing a SIMPLE 401(K), so if your employer offers a SIMPLE 401(k), don't assume that you will have all the features of a traditional 401(k).

TRUTH

3

Increasing tax brackets

The good news is that with a traditional IRA or traditional 401(k), your investments grow tax deferred until you take money out of the account. While anything you take out is subject to income tax, the rest continues to grow on a tax-deferred basis. Because tax deferral is considered such a good thing, many people put off taking anything out of their traditional IRAs or traditional 401(k)s until they reach the age of 70 1/2, at which time the law requires you to begin to take money from these accounts. The minimum amount that you must take each year, once you have reached the age of 70 1/2, is easily determined by using simple IRS charts. (How often do you see the words IRS and simple in the same sentence?) These charts are based primarily on your life expectancy. It is very important that, once you reach the age of 70 1/2, you take out at least your minimum required distribution amount annually, because if you fail to do so, you will be assessed a penalty by the IRS equal to 50% of the amount you failed to take that, by law, you should have taken.

The bad news is that too much of a good thing, even tax deferral, is not necessarily a good thing.

When you withdraw money from a traditional IRA or a traditional 401(k), you are required to pay income taxes on the money that you withdraw at your ordinary income tax rates that presently can be as high as 35%. And therein lies the rub. One of the assumptions upon which many people operate is that when they retire and start to take money out of their traditional IRA or traditional 401(k), they will be

Too much of a good thing, even tax deferral, is not necessarily a good thing.

in a lower tax rate. Ignoring the possibility of changes in the law's increasing tax rates, if you wait until you are 70 1/2 to start taking your initial distributions from your traditional IRA or traditional 401(k), you run the definite risk that the substantial minimum required distributions you must then start to take will bump you into a higher tax bracket and thereby subject the money you take out to significantly higher taxes. It seems you are damned if you do and damned if you don't. On the one hand, waiting until the latest possible time to start taking your minimum required distributions permits you to prolong the advantages of income tax deferral. However, by waiting that long to begin taking your minimum required distributions, you are in danger of wiping out a significant portion of your gain by having the money you take out be subject to higher income tax rates.

But there is a solution.

Although you must start to take distributions from your traditional IRA or traditional 401(k) by the time that you reach the age of 70 1/2, you are permitted to withdraw money from your traditional IRA or traditional 401(k) without any kind of penalty for early withdrawal after the age of 59 1/2. Therefore, you may want to consider taking some money out of your traditional IRA or traditional 401(k) on a regular basis between the ages of 59 1/2 and 70 1/2 to avoid the problem of having to take too

Once you've converted your traditional IRA to a Roth IRA, all the growth of the wide range of investments available to you in your Roth IRA is not just tax deferred; it is totally tax free.

much out if you delay starting your withdrawals until the age of 70 1/2. An advantage of utilizing this strategy is that you will have total control over determining how much you can safely take out without suffering the additional financial setback of having the amount of your withdrawal put you into a higher ordinary income tax bracket.

On the other hand, if you employ this strategy, you will have lost the advantage of further tax deferral on the amounts that you withdraw before the age of 70 1/2. Or have you?

You can always take the money that you withdraw and invest in tax-advantaged investments such as tax-free municipal bonds and thereby provide for not just tax-deferred, but even tax-free growth. But an even greater opportunity may be presented to you by, instead of merely taking a direct distribution of some of your traditional IRA, you convert a portion of your traditional IRA into a Roth IRA. At such time that you convert a traditional IRA to a Roth IRA, you must pay ordinary income taxes on the amount that you convert. However, once you've converted your traditional IRA to a Roth IRA, all the growth of the wide range of investments available to you in your Roth IRA is not just tax deferred; it is totally tax free. Until 2010, to convert a traditional IRA to a Roth IRA, your income (coupled with that of your spouse's if you are married and filing a joint return) must be less than $100,000. Beginning in 2010, the income limitation on Roth IRA conversions will be eliminated, so even if your income now does not permit you to do such a conversion, this option will be available to you regardless of your income starting in 2010.

In fact, there is an added inducement to doing such a conversion in 2010, because the IRS will permit you to spread out the income tax payments required due to the conversion over the next two years rather than making the entire amount due in the tax year that the conversion occurs. It also is important to remember that, when doing a conversion from a traditional IRA to a Roth IRA, you have the option of converting as much or as little of your traditional IRA as you wish. Therefore, once again, you put yourself in the position of being much more able to control any possible bump up in your ordinary income tax rate bracket by only converting such amounts that you are confident will not significantly increase your tax burden by putting you into a higher ordinary income tax rate bracket. In fact, there is nothing that prevents you from spreading out a total conversion of your traditional IRA to a Roth IRA over a number of years to achieve greater income tax efficiency.

TRUTH

40

Suing plan administrators

It is rare for the justices of the Supreme Court to agree on anything, but in 2008 they unanimously agreed that workers had the right to sue the administrators of their company 401(k) plan for losses in their individual 401(k) accounts due to the negligence of the plan administrators.

Federal law requires the administrators of 401(k) plans to manage the funds as "prudent experts" on behalf of the participants in the plan. What it means to be a prudent expert is constantly open to interpretation, but lawsuits have been filed for a number of reasons, including providing poor investment choices, charging unreasonably high management fees, or in the case of James LaRue, the plaintiff in the Supreme Court case, failing to promptly follow the instructions of the 401(k) participant to switch investments to safer alternatives. In LaRue's case, he alleged that the value of his 401(k) dropped by $150,000 when plan administrators failed to follow his instructions in 2001 and 2002 to switch his 401(k) investment into lower-risk investment options.

The decision should not have come as too much of a surprise to the investment management community, because federal law has long permitted lawsuits by participants in traditional defined benefit retirement plans against plan administrators for breaching their fiduciary duty to the plan participants through negligence or misdeeds that cause losses to the plan. However, the plan administrators had pinned their hopes on a technical interpretation of the law, arguing that the law and prior court rulings only pertained to traditional defined benefit pension plans where any misdeeds by administrators would affect the entire plan as contrasted to the situation with a 401(k) plan, where they argued that even if they might have been considered to have acted improperly, their actions did not affect the plan itself, but only, as in LaRue's case, a particular employee's account within the plan. This nitpicking reasoning did not

A large number of lawsuits against 401(k) plan administrators have involved accusations of excessive management and administration fees.

hold much weight with the Supreme Court Justices. In the Court's opinion, Justice John Paul Stevens wrote, "Fiduciary misconduct need not threaten the solvency of the entire plan to reduce benefits below the amount that participants would otherwise receive." In a concurring opinion, Justice Clarence Thomas noted that a loss sustained by any individual's account effectively was a loss for the plan as a whole. The Supreme Court ruling overturned the decision of the 4th U.S. Circuit Court of Appeals, which had ruled in favor of the plan administrators.

A possible fly in the ointment, however, could be found in the concurring opinion of Chief Justice John Roberts, who, although he voted to permit LaRue to be able to sue the plan administrator, raised the possibility that the plan administrator might have been in a better position to defend the case it if had required the plan participant to exhaust his administrative

> Investing for your retirement in a 401(k) plan is not something that should be done on automatic pilot and without constant vigilance.

remedies before taking the case to court. Whether this will serve as a roadmap for 401(k) administrators accused of wrongdoing to stall resolution of claims against them remains to be seen.

The real lesson here is not that the courts are a good place to take a claim for mismanagement against a 401(k) plan administrator, but that investing for your retirement in a 401(k) plan is not something that should be done on automatic pilot and without constant vigilance. As always, what you make from any investment is not as important as what you get to keep. The size of the fees that you pay in your 401(k) plan can have a serious effect on the ultimate success or failure of your retirement plan. A large number of lawsuits against 401(k) plan administrators have involved accusations of excessive management and administration fees. Some cases have also challenged fee-sharing arrangement between the mutual fund companies who supply the investment vehicles for the 401(k) plan and the plan administrators. Federal law not only requires that all fees be reasonable but also that they be fully and adequately disclosed. Unfortunately, from the plethora of lawsuits, it would appear that many companies have fee structures that, at best, are confusing and hard to understand, and at worst, are illegal, excessive, and undisclosed.

It is the obligation of every 401(k) plan investor to make sure that he understands fully what fees and administrative costs are involved in his plan, so he can make rational investing decisions as well as join with other plan participants to urge the company to utilize plan administrators who provide good service, good investment options, and a reasonable and clearly disclosed fee structure.

Fees may have a significant effect on the performance of your investments, but inevitably the choices you make regarding what investments you use in your 401(k) are of paramount importance. The array of choices is impressive and mind boggling to many, from money market funds, stable value accounts, and stock mutual funds to bond mutual funds. As always, the higher the risk of a particular investment, the potentially higher the return, but this does not mean that most people can afford to be too conservative and invest solely in money market funds or other low-risk investments. The best thing you can do is make sure that the investment choices in your 401(k) are part of a properly diversified portfolio that considers what you will need for retirement, how long it will be until you retire, and your tolerance for risk. Once you have made the allocation of your 401(k) investment dollars among the various investment choices available to you, your decision making is not done. Although it rarely makes sense (or many dollars) to continually trade your account, seeking the winning investments of the moment, it also does not make sense to just make an initial investment choice and leave it alone. Regularly review investment portfolios inside and outside of a 401(k), perhaps annually, to make sure that your investment strategy is still in place.

TRUTH

41

Retirement savings contribution credit

Sometimes a good thing just gets better. Such is the situation with the Retirement Savings Contributions Credit, also known as the Savers Credit. It has been around since 2002, but many people are still unaware of it and are missing out on a tremendous tax break.

We all know (at least after having read this book) how important it is to save for retirement in an IRA or a 401(k) or both. The federal government has passed numerous laws both to encourage people to invest for their future in IRAs and 401(k)s and to make the process as easy as possible. But the Retirement Savings Contributions Credit is more than just a simplification of the process, such as when employers were permitted to make enrollment in company 401(k) plans automatic. The Retirement Savings Contributions Credit actually puts as much as $2,000 in your pocket by reducing your income tax burden by that amount.

Tax deductions, such as what you get when you make a tax-deductible contribution to an IRA or a pretax payment to a 401(k), reduce the amount of your income that is subject to income tax. In the case of tax-deductible contributions to a traditional IRA and pretax payments to a traditional 401(k), the amount that is contributed to your traditional IRA or 401(k) is not subject to income tax when it goes into your retirement account. Instead, it is allowed to grow unhampered by income taxes until you withdraw the money from your traditional IRA or 401(k).

But a tax credit is different. Tax credits are more valuable than tax deductions because, while a tax deduction may lower the amount of your income that is subject to income taxes, a tax credit represents a dollar-for-dollar reduction in your actual income taxes. So, for example, with a $2,000 tax credit, which is the maximum amount under the Retirement Savings Contributions Credit program, your income tax bill is reduced by $2,000.

The Retirement Savings Contributions Credit actually puts as much as $2,000 in your pocket by reducing your income tax burden by that amount.

Under the terms and conditions of the Retirement Savings Contributions Credit law, if you meet certain income and other guidelines, you will be able to take as a tax credit between 10% and 50% of as much as $4,000 that you contribute to specific retirement plans, including a traditional IRA, Roth IRA, or 401(k). In fact, if, as some people do, you contribute the maximum amount you can to an IRA and a 401(k), those amounts can be added together to determine the amount of your contributions to which the credit rate of between 10% and 50% will apply. In addition, if you are making a tax-deductible contribution to a traditional IRA or a pretax payment to a traditional 401(k), you can get the tax credit on top of the benefits of having your contribution be tax-deductible or pretax.

> The tax credit ranges from 10% to 50%, with the highest credit ranges applying to the lowest earning taxpayers.

To qualify for the credit you must have been born before January 2, 1990. You also may not be a full-time student and may not be claimed as an exemption by your parents or anyone else on their income tax return.

The amount of your modified adjusted gross income used to determine your eligibility for the credit is indexed for inflation each year. The most modified adjusted gross income that a married couple filing jointly may have and be eligible for some of the credit was $53,000 in 2008. The most modified adjusted gross income that a person filing as head of household may have and qualify for some of the tax credit was $39,750 in 2008. The most modified adjusted gross income that a person filing as single or married filing separately may have and qualify for some of the tax credit was $26,500 in 2008. For most people, the amount of their modified adjusted gross income is found on line 38 of their Form 1040.

The tax credit ranges from 10% to 50%, with the highest credit ranges applying to the lowest earning taxpayers. The maximum amount of your annual contributions to the covered retirement plans to which the tax credit rate is applied is $2,000 person. For example, if Homer and Marge filed a joint income tax return showing modified adjusted gross income of $30,000 and Homer contributed $4,000 to an IRA and $4,000 to a 401(k), he would have made total qualifying contributions of $8,000. However, the maximum amount that the credit is based on is $2,000 per person, so $4,000 is the figure against which, in Homer and Marge's case, the highest tax credit rate of 50% is applied, thereby providing them with a tax credit of $2,000, which is a lot of doughnuts. Single individuals are eligible for as much as a $1,000 tax credit if they meet the income and other guidelines.

The exact amount of the credit is calculated on Form 8880. Once you have determined the amount of the tax credit you are entitled to, you report the credit on line 53 of your Form 1040 or line 33 of your Form 1040A and attach a copy of Form 8880 to your income tax return.

TRUTH

42

Divorce and your IRA or 401(k)

In many divorces, the most significant assets are the retirement accounts, particularly IRAs and 401(k)s. Avoiding the pitfalls when dividing 401(k) accounts and IRAs is an important part of the financial planning that should go into any divorce.

IRA

It is common for someone to be ordered to give a portion of her IRA to her soon-to-be-former spouse as a part of the divorce judgment. Often the IRA is divided equally. The laws present an opportunity for avoiding unnecessary income taxes when dividing an IRA.

To avoid unnecessary taxes, first and foremost the division of the IRA must be required by the terms of the divorce judgment that the court issued. Most divorces involve a settlement agreed on by the divorcing husband and wife. In that instance, their agreement is incorporated into the order of the court. If the divorcing couple is unable to agree on the terms of their divorce, a judge must issue an order after a trial. In either event, it is important to specifically deal with the IRA by making it a part of the negotiated settlement agreement that becomes part of the judge's order or by presenting proper evidence to the judge to enable him to make a proper determination regarding the IRA in his order.

A second important condition for avoiding income taxes on the division of an IRA at the time of a divorce is to make sure that the division of the IRA is done by way of a trustee-to-trustee transfer. For example, if you are going to be giving your divorcing spouse half of your IRA, make sure that the funds are transferred to him by the trustee of your IRA directly to the trustee of your soon-to-be-former spouse's IRA. If he does not have an IRA, he should open one to receive the funds to be transferred. If you make the mistake of taking

> A divorce can be bad enough. There's no need to make it an even more taxing event by failing to follow a few simple steps when splitting up IRA or 401(k) assets.

the funds out of your IRA and then writing a check to your ex-spouse, regardless of whether he deposits that check into an IRA on his behalf, you will be hit with income taxes on the money withdrawn from your IRA. Of course, these rules would not apply if you were dividing a Roth IRA, which generally does not carry tax consequences upon withdrawal of funds. However, it is still a good practice to have any division of even the assets in a Roth IRA done as a direct trustee-to-trustee transfer.

> A significant pitfall to avoid is the transfer of IRA funds to a divorcing spouse before your divorce is ordered by the court or without a provision for the transfer specifically being contained within the judgment of divorce issued by the court.

A significant pitfall to avoid is the transfer of IRA funds to a divorcing spouse before your divorce is ordered by the court or without a provision for the transfer specifically being contained within the judgment of divorce issued by the court. In either of these events, not only would you lose the money in your IRA, but you would also be responsible for income taxes on the amount of the traditional IRA transferred to your soon-to-be ex-spouse. And, to make matters worse, if you are under the age of 59 1/2 at the time that you make the transfer to your soon-to-be-ex-spouse without a court order that specifically provides for the transfer of your traditional IRA funds, you will also be required to pay an excise tax penalty of 10% on the amount transferred as a premature withdrawal.

The magic words that should appear in any divorce judgment that involves dividing IRA money are the "transfer of the IRA funds are required by the terms of the judgment as a division of property and is intended to be done as a tax-free transfer pursuant to Section 408(d)(6) of the Internal Revenue Code." If you do this, and you make sure that the transfer is accomplished by a transfer directly from your IRA to your ex-spouse's IRA, you will be able to avoid income taxes on the transfer.

401(k)

Although, as with an IRA, the law requires that the provisions for any division of the 401(k) account specifically be included in the divorce judgment of the court and the actual transfer be done by a trustee-to-trustee transfer, additional requirements are present with the division of a 401(k) account to avoid unnecessary taxes.

First, the judge issuing the divorce judgment must sign a special order of the court referred to as a Qualified Domestic Relations Order (QDRO). The QDRO legally establishes the right of the ex-spouse, referred to in this case as the "alternate payee" to receive a division of the 401(k) assets and to become responsible for income taxes incurred in regard to those assets. As with an IRA being divided, the funds should be transferred directly from the trustee of the 401(k) plan to be divided to the trustee of an IRA on behalf of the spouse receiving those funds. This will avoid income taxes and withholding taxes being assessed on the transfer. Without a proper QDRO, the 401(k) plan administrator would be required to withhold 20% of the amount being transferred for income taxes. It is important to transfer the funds from the 401(k) account to the ex-spouse's IRA within 60 days to comply with federal law.

QDROs are complicated documents. Plan administrators are quite particular (some would say downright picky) as to the specific language that must appear in QDROs that pertain to their plan's assets. It is always a good practice for your lawyer to ask your 401(k) plan administrator if she has a model QDRO form that she prefers. If this is the case, your lawyer should use that form and, upon completion of the form, present it to the judge involved in the divorce case for his signature.

A divorce can be bad enough. There's no need to make it an even more taxing event by failing to follow a few simple steps when splitting up IRA or 401(k) assets.

TRUTH

43

Health savings accounts

A Health Savings Account (HSA) is a tax-advantaged way to provide for the payment of medical bills while potentially providing another tax-advantaged way to save for retirement similar to a traditional IRA.

HSAs are the new kid on the block, but they appear to have more staying power than the boy band The New Kids on the Block. The law permitting HSAs has only been around since 2003, and many people are still unaware of the many advantages of HSAs. People under the age of 65 who purchase medical insurance with a high deductible amount—which for 2008 was at least $1,100 for single person coverage and at least $2,200 for a family policy—are eligible for an HSA. A person with an HSA can make a tax-deductible contribution of as much as $2,900 for an individual policy or $5,800 for a family policy. People who are 55 or over can make an additional deductible contribution of $900 to their HSA, whether it is an individual policy or a family policy. An additional benefit to the use of a HSA coupled with a high-deductible medical insurance policy is that the premium for the medical insurance policy is generally less than more traditional health insurance policies.

The money that you put into your HSA is invested, as with an IRA. In a way, you can consider the HSA a hybrid of the traditional IRA and the Roth IRA. If you take money out of your HSA to pay for qualified medical expenses, which can include required deductible payments or certain medical expenses not covered by your medical insurance, such as nonprescription medicines (even aspirin), you are not required to pay income tax on the withdrawal, similar to a Roth IRA distribution. On the other hand, if you withdraw money from your HSA for nonmedical reasons, the amount of your withdrawal is not only subject to income taxes, but also a 10% penalty. However, withdrawals for any reason by HSA owners who are either disabled or at least 65 years old are subject to income tax but not the 10% penalty, making the withdrawal similar to a timely distribution from a traditional IRA. In

For young, healthy individuals, an HSA may represent a cost-effective way to pay for both health care and retirement.

this situation, the money invested in your HSA has been growing and compounding on a tax-deferred basis just like contributions to a traditional IRA. The amounts that you contribute to your HSA, even though they eventually may be used in the fashion of a traditional IRA, do not reduce your ability to contribute the maximum amount to a traditional or Roth IRA.

Young, healthy people are particularly well suited to use an HSA as a way not only to provide for their health care costs in a tax-advantaged manner, but also as a way to possibly contribute more money to grow tax deferred for retirement. Over time, if your medical expenses are low and you make regular contributions to the account, you will have created another valuable tax-deferred retirement savings vehicle.

> If your medical expenses are low and you make regular contributions to the account, you will have created another valuable tax-deferred retirement savings vehicle.

Even though you may not set up or contribute to an HSA once you have reached the age of 65, you can still use the money for your medical expenses tax free and without penalty. In addition, if you withdraw the money at age 65 or later for nonmedical reasons, you only are required to pay income taxes on the amount of your withdrawal, just like a timely withdrawal from a traditional IRA. As with a traditional IRA, until you do take out your money from your HSA, your money will have been growing and compounding tax deferred, which is a significant advantage.

IRAs and HSAs are also connected by your ability to fund your HSA with money transferred from your IRA. This can be accomplished by a transfer from the trustee of your IRA to the trustee of your HSA. Regardless of your age when you do this transfer, it will not be subject to income taxes, as would other distributions from an IRA. The maximum amount that you can transfer from your IRA to your HSA is limited to the maximum annual contribution amount, which in 2008 is $2,900 for an individual plan and $5,800 for a family plan. Note that this transfer of funds from your IRA to your HSA may only be done once.

Although you may open an HSA on your own, some employers are now offering HSAs as an employer-sponsored health insurance option. In an effort to encourage their use, some employers are even paying for some or all of the cost. Certain employers even offer a 401(k)-like matching contribution. If your employer provides a high-deductible health insurance policy, you may be able to make your contribution, if any, to the premium as a pretax contribution. If you open an HSA on your own, the money you contribute is deductible on your income taxes. Either way, the result is a tax saving to you, although if the funding of your HSA is done through a pretax contribution through your employer, you end up saving FICA and FUTA tax money.

If you establish an HSA through your employer and then leave your job for whatever reason, you can keep the money in the HSA and still use that money to pay for qualified medical expenses without incurring income taxes. However, if you use the money for nonmedical reasons before you reach the age of 65, you will be subject to income tax on the amount of the withdrawal as well as a 10% penalty.

Individuals or families with high regular medical expenses or who will have difficulty meeting the terms of their deductible payments are not well suited for HSAs. Neither are families with young children who may require more regular medical care likely to find an HSA helpful. But particularly for young, healthy individuals, an HSA may represent a cost-effective way to pay for both health care and retirement.

TRUTH

44

Unmarried and same sex couples

Many people have chosen to live together without getting married. Some are same-sex couples who, except in Massachusetts and California, are not permitted by law to marry, while others are opposite-sex couples who have chosen, for whatever reason, not to marry. All these people must pay particular attention to the rules regarding inheriting of 401(k)s and IRAs to make sure that their wishes are followed.

Complicating things even further are the situations in the few states that still recognize common law marriages, where a couple that lives together and holds themselves out to the public as being married for a significant but unspecified period of time may be considered married under the laws of that state. Presently, the following states recognize common law marriages in some manner or another:

Alabama

Colorado

Georgia (if created before 1/1/97)

Idaho (if created before 1/1/96)

Iowa

Kansas

Montana

New Hampshire (for inheritance purposes only)

Ohio (if created before 10/10/91)

Oklahoma

Pennsylvania

Rhode Island

South Carolina

Texas

Utah

> Make sure that your 401(k) or IRA will pass to the people you wish to inherit these assets by ensuring that you name them in your beneficiary designation.

Although the federal government does not recognize same-sex marriages, it recognizes opposite-sex common law marriages for purposes of inheriting an IRA or a 401(k). However, this area of the law is particularly tricky, and any common law married couple should consult their lawyers to make sure that the beneficiary designations for their 401(k) and IRA are in order to feel confident that they will get all the tax and financial benefits that they may be entitled to.

In a 401(k) plan, your spouse is automatically named as your primary beneficiary; however, if you are married under the common law or you are a member of an unmarried couple either same sex or opposite sex, make sure that your beneficiary designation specifically names your spouse or partner, if that is your desire. Until the enactment of the Pension Protection Act of 2006, only a spouse who inherited a 401(k) had the right to roll over the inherited 401(k) into an IRA. Now, however, any named beneficiary of a 401(k) has the right to roll the 401(k) into an IRA and make withdrawals based on his own life expectancy. As always, it is crucial to have an up-to-date beneficiary designation in place, because if you do not and your 401(k) ends up passing to your estate, the 401(k) has to come out in as few as five years after your death, and the ability to continue tax-deferred compounding with a traditional 401(k) or tax-free compounding with a Roth 401(k) is lost.

As for IRAs, the law also permits nonspouses to roll over inherited IRAs into an IRA and permits the nonspouse beneficiary to continue the tax-deferred compounding with a traditional IRA or tax-free compounding with a Roth IRA over the lifetime of the designated beneficiary. Again, however, the risk of losing that ability to continue tax-deferred or tax-free compounding can be lost, and the funds will have to be withdrawn in as little as five years if a proper beneficiary designation is not in order.

The biggest problem facing unmarried couples whether they are same sex or opposite sex couples when it comes to inheriting a 401(k) or an IRA occurs when the deceased 401(k) owner or IRA owner dies without having a Will or an up-to-date beneficiary designation. In that case, the laws of intestacy dictate that the 401(k) and IRA pass to the heirs at law, as determined by the state. This means that the person the 401(k) or IRA owner most likely would have wanted to inherit her 401(k) or IRA

People don't plan to fail, but all too many fail to plan.

will not. Rather, these assets will pass to people who may be the most remote of relatives of the deceased 401(k) or IRA owner.

Make sure that your 401(k) or IRA will pass to the people you wish to inherit these assets by ensuring that you name them in your beneficiary designation. It is equally important when it comes to assets that do not have a designated beneficiary to make sure that you have a properly executed Will by which you can provide for the passing of your assets to the specific people you want. People don't plan to fail, but all too many fail to plan.

TRUTH

45

Steve's rules, part 1

"Retirement is not a vicarious experience," —Marian Yunghaus

When it comes to retirement, the decisions you make earlier in life can go a long way in determining your financial success or failure in retirement and the quality of your retirement experience. Knowing and following a few simple rules can help you make good decisions when it comes to using IRAs and 401(k)s toward a rewarding retirement.

Rule 1: Take your minimum required distributions on time—Many people lose track of when they are required to take their Minimum Required Distributions from their traditional IRAs and traditional 401(k)s. If you're late in taking your initial withdrawals, you'll be charged serious penalties. As you approach your seventieth birthday (and hopefully well before then), you should have a plan for how you'll most effectively take your Minimum Required Distributions, with an eye toward the income tax ramifications of delaying your first payment to the latest possible time and having to take two distributions in one year.

In addition, in any year that you fail to take your Minimum Required Distribution, you can be subject to a heavy tax penalty, so make sure you keep track of your required distributions.

Rule 2: If you haven't paid attention to Rule 1, make sure that you file an IRS Form 5329—Even if you did not take your Minimum Required Distribution in a timely fashion, you can always argue to the IRS that your failure was a "reasonable error," correct the problem, and take the required distribution. File a Form 5329 and request a refund of your 50% excess accumulation tax. Include a letter of explanation, and do your best to be persuasive. You've got nothing to lose.

Rule 3: If you leave a job, don't cash out your 401(k)—When you leave your job, you can leave your 401(k) at your company, roll it over into an IRA, roll it over into your new employer's 401(k), or take the money and run. The first three options will continue your retirement planning. The last will require you to pay income taxes, stop your tax-deferred growth, and even subject you to a large tax penalty if you are younger than 59 1/2.

Rule 4: Don't borrow from your 401(k) unless you absolutely have to do so—Borrowing from your 401(k) defeats the purpose of the account, limits the amount of growth in the account for retirement, and carries risks of penalties. No one should borrow from their 401(k) unless they have fully explored other options, such as a home equity loan where the interest can be tax deductible.

Rule 5: Make sure that the Beneficiary Designations of your 401(k)s and IRAs are in good order—Make sure your Beneficiary Designation is current and reflects any changes you might want to make as to who will be your beneficiaries due to marriages, births, deaths, or divorces.

Rule 6: Make sure that the Beneficiary Designations of your 401(k)s and IRAs have contingent beneficiaries—To provide the maximum flexibility and enable you to take the fullest advantage of the rules permitting Stretch IRAs, your Beneficiary Designations must contain the names of contingent beneficiaries.

Rule 7: Reduce the fees that you pay in your 401(k) and IRA as much as possible—The amounts that you pay in various fees for the management of your 401(k) and IRA as well as other services you are billed for in your retirement accounts has a significant effect on what your money will earn for you. Make sure that you understand all the fees you are paying, and take the steps necessary, where possible, to reduce them.

Rule 8: Don't rely on automatic enrollment in your company's 401(k) plan—If you are automatically enrolled in your company's 401(k) plan, the amounts that you contribute and the investments that form the basis of your 401(k) are determined by default. These decisions may not be the ones you would make. Enrollment in a 401(k) plan, whether done automatically or intentionally, is good. But it is a better when you make informed decisions as to how much money you'll be investing and where you'll be investing it.

Rule 9: A Roth IRA generally is better than a Traditional IRA—No generalization is worth a damn, including this one, but for most people, the benefits of a Roth IRA are greater than a Traditional IRA.

Rule 10: A Traditional 401(k) is better than a Roth IRA if your employer provides matching contributions—There are many fees involved with a traditional IRA, over which you have little or no control, that can limit the growth of your 401(k). With a Roth IRA, you are in a much better position to pick your investments and control your fees. However, if your employer provides matching contributions to your Traditional 401(k), that is free money that tips the scales in favor of a traditional 401(k) over a Roth IRA.

Rule 11: Pay off your credit cards before you invest in any retirement plan other than a Traditional 401(k) that has employer matching contributions—You will get more bang for your bucks if you pay off your high-interest credit cards before saving for retirement with the one exception of investing in a traditional 401(k) that provides you with the free money of employer matching contributions.

Rule 12: Never invest more than 10% of the value of your 401(k) in your own company's stock—It doesn't make sense to put all your investment eggs in one stock basket regardless of the company. The fact that you work for a particular company already means that you're invested in it. Think Enron. To additionally put a large portion of your 401(k) dollars into the same company's stock is just too risky.

Rule 13: Customize your IRA or 401(k) Beneficiary Designation as necessary to have it most accurately reflect your estate and financial plan—To have your Beneficiary Designation be a part of your estate and financial plan, you may have to customize the form to make sure that your wishes are clearly indicated and your options preserved.

TRUTH

46

Steve's rules, part 2

Rule 14: Make sure that your heirs are aware of their ability to use qualified disclaimers—A qualified disclaimer when coupled with a properly completed Beneficiary Designation opens the possibilities of many years of tax savings through the use of Stretch IRAs.

Rule 15: Have a Durable Power of Attorney—A Durable Power of Attorney is a document by which you appoint someone to act on your behalf in financial matters. It is particularly helpful if you are incapacitated and need to change your Beneficiary Designation or make a Disclaimer.

Rule 16: The investment choices that you make within your IRA and 401(k) should be part of an overall asset allocation strategy—A proper asset allocation strategy is the best way to control risk and seek a good return on your retirement investment dollars. The investment choices that you make in your IRA and 401(k) should be part of an overall asset allocation strategy.

Rule 17: Never transfer IRA or 401(k) funds to a divorcing spouse before the court issues an order of divorce—If you transfer IRA funds to a spouse you are in the process of divorcing prior to the court issuing an order of divorce or without a provision for the transfer of those assets specifically being contained with the divorce judgment, you will be subject to severe tax penalties.

Rule 18: If you are 50 or over, take advantage of catch-up provisions that permit you to contribute more to your 401(k) or IRA—The law permits people who are at least 50 years old to make additional contributions to their IRAs and 401(k)s that younger people are not allowed to do. Whenever possible, take advantage of this favor that Congress is doing for you.

Rule 19: Correct any excess contributions you may have made to a Roth IRA as quickly as possible—If you made too large a contribution to a Roth IRA or did not qualify for a Roth IRA but made a contribution, the law permits you to correct this with minimal problems. However, if you fail to correct this mistake in a timely manner, you will be subject to a large excise tax penalty.

Rule 20: If you are young and healthy, you should consider a Health Savings Account—Young, healthy people may find a Health Savings Account (HAS) an effective way to save both for health care and their retirement.

Rule 21: Consider the effects of delaying to the last moment withdrawals from your Traditional 401(k) or Traditional IRA—If you wait until the last possible moment to start taking your withdrawals from your Traditional 401(k) or Traditional IRA, you may unnecessarily increase your income tax burden. Do your homework, and consider taking regular withdrawals earlier and investing the money in tax-advantaged investments such as municipal bonds or converting to a Roth IRA.

Rule 22: Consider a SEP IRA, SIMPLE IRA, SIMPLE 401(k), or an Individual 401(k) if you are self-employed—All these options are available to you to help you plan for retirement if you are self-employed. All of them have advantages and disadvantages, so you should compare them carefully and determine what is best for you.

Rule 23: Consider converting your traditional IRA to a Roth IRA—Converting your traditional IRA to a Roth IRA in a properly timed manner can provide you with all the benefits of a Roth IRA, including greater flexibility and control over your retirement funds.

Rule 24: As you approach retirement, consider the effects of IRA distributions on the taxability of your Social Security benefits—The money that you receive from your minimum required distributions from a traditional IRA may affect the taxability of your Social Security benefits. Roth IRA distributions do not affect the taxability of your Social Security benefits. Plan early to deal with this possibility. A Roth IRA conversion may be in order.

Rule 25: If you meet the income guidelines, take the Retirement Savings Contributions Credit—Income tax credits provide a dollar-for-dollar reduction of the amount you are required to pay in income taxes. Always make sure you're getting every credit you're entitled to. The Retirement Savings Contribution Credit can be worth as much as $2,000 to you.

Rule 26: Consider setting up a Roth IRA for children or grandchildren as young as seven years old—A Roth IRA established for a child who is paid for legitimately performing services can be an astonishingly tremendous savings vehicle.

Rule 27: If you're interested in investing your IRA money in types of investments not usually contained in conventional IRAs, consider setting up a Self-Directed IRA—A Self-Directed IRA permits you to put your IRA money into investments such as real estate, stocks and bonds of privately owned companies, and even race horses. If that is your cup of tea (or oats), you should consider a Self-Directed IRA.

Rule 28: If you are married and qualify, set up a Spousal IRA—Even if your spouse is not working outside of the home, you may be eligible for the considerable benefits of a Spousal IRA.

Rule 29: If you have a Roth 401(k), roll it into a Roth IRA at retirement—A quirk in the law requires people who have Roth 401(k) accounts to take mandatory distributions at age 70 1/2. However, you can avoid these mandatory withdrawals by rolling over your Roth 401(k) account to a Roth IRA.

Rule 30: A trust is a good beneficiary for an IRA where young children would otherwise directly inherit the money—A trust is a good way to provide the benefits of an IRA to a person who might inherit your IRA but may be too young to handle the money or otherwise needs the protection of a trust.

Rule 31: Don't leave a job until you're sure what the vesting requirements are for your 401(k)—Although this should not be the sole determining factor as to whether you leave a job, leaving a job just short of being vested in your employer's contributions to your 401(k) can cost you a lot of money.

TRUTH

4/

Definitions

Sometimes the terms used with IRAs and 401(k)s are confusing. Other times they seem to be written in code. Often, they are—the Internal Revenue Code. Either way, it's helpful to understand the meaning of the many words and acronyms that you'll encounter.

12b-1 fee—A continuing fee that many mutual funds charge to the holders of mutual funds to cover advertising and marketing expenses. Some mutual funds proclaim that they are "no load" but still charge 12b-1 fees.

401(k)—A type of employer-sponsored retirement program that takes its name from the authorizing section of the Internal Revenue Code. It is a defined contribution plan.

Actively managed mutual fund—A mutual fund to which you pay a fee for the mutual fund managers to do research and actively buy and sell stocks.

Adjusted Gross Income (AGI)—The figure upon which a person's income tax liability is based. It is determined by taking a person's income after specific adjustments have been made but prior to applying the standard or itemized deduction and personal exemptions that may apply.

After-Tax Income—Money upon which you have already paid income taxes that you may use to fund a retirement account, such as a Roth IRA.

Asset allocation—The process of dividing investment dollars among different classes of assets, such as stocks and bonds, to achieve a balance of growth and risk.

Beneficiary Designation form—The form by which the owner of a retirement plan indicates who will inherit the account if he dies while the retirement account still contains assets.

Compound growth—This occurs when the earnings from your investments are reinvested and generate their own earnings that in turn are reinvested and generate even further earnings. When compound growth is either tax free, as in a Roth IRA or tax deferred, as in a traditional IRA, the growth that occurs is dramatic.

Defined Benefit Plan—A type of retirement plan in which the employer contributes all the money that is put into the plan on behalf of employees. The amount of the retirement benefit that the employee receives is a specific amount that is not directly based on the performance of the underlying investments.

Defined Contribution Plan—The dominant type of employer-sponsored retirement program today that is funded with contributions of employees and/or the employer. The amount that the employee receives at retirement depends on the performance of the underlying investments in the employee's plan.

Disclaimer—A written renunciation of the right to receive property, such as by the primary beneficiary of an IRA following the death of the owner of the IRA. Following a disclaimer, the property passes to the contingent beneficiary as indicated in the Beneficiary Designation.

Durable Power of Attorney—A document by which a person appoints someone to act on her behalf in financial matters.

Earned income—Income that is countable for determining eligibility to contribute to a retirement plan, such as a traditional IRA or a Roth IRA. For IRA purposes, wages, self-employment income, and alimony constitute earned income, but interest, dividends, Social Security payments, and pension payments are not considered as earned income.

Excess contribution—The amount by which a contribution to an IRA is greater than the amount allowed by law.

FICA—The acronym for Federal Insurance Contributions Act. This represents the tax deducted from a person's wages for Social Security and Medicare.

FUTA—The acronym for the Federal Unemployment Tax Act. This is a tax paid by employers for the administration of unemployment benefits.

Head of Household—A tax filing status (such as single, married filing jointly, or married filing separately) that applies to a person who is either married or unmarried but maintains a household for a dependent and provides more than half of the dependent's support.

Health Savings Account—A tax-advantaged medical savings account that can function similarly to an IRA.

Individual 401(k)—Also known as a Solo 401(k), this is a type of 401(k) used primarily for self-employed individuals.

IRA—An acronym that, depending on the context, can refer to an Individual Retirement Account, the Intercollegiate Rowing Association, or the Irish Republican Army. For our purposes, an IRA is a tax-advantaged retirement account for individuals, which comes in a number of different variations.

Limited Liability Company (LLC)—A simplified form of a business entity similar to a corporation that is often appropriate for small businesses. It limits personal liability on behalf of the people involved in the business and provides certain tax benefits.

Load mutual fund—A mutual fund that charges a fee when the investor either buys shares in the fund (front-end load) or sells shares of the fund (back-end load).

Marital Deduction—A provision of the estate tax law that permits spouses, at death, to pass their property to their surviving spouse tax free.

Married Filing Jointly—A tax filing status for married people who choose to file a joint income tax return. It is often the most advantageous way for a married couple to file their tax returns.

Married Filing Separately—A tax filing status for married people in which each chooses to file a separate tax return. This particular tax filing status is not favored in many retirement planning laws.

Minimum Required Distribution (MRD)—The smallest amount that you are required by law to withdraw from your Traditional IRA or Traditional 401(k) upon retirement once you reach the age of 70 1/2. Roth IRAs and Roth 401(k)s do not have minimum required distribution amounts for their initial owners.

Modified Adjusted Gross Income (MAGI)—This is calculated by adding to an individual's adjusted gross income certain items such as student loan deductions and IRA contribution deductions.

Passively managed mutual fund—A mutual fund, such as an Index fund, that reflects a specific stock market index, such as the S & P 500. Little trading is done by the mutual fund, and the fees are considerably lower than actively managed funds.

Pretax income—Money that is subtracted from an employee's wages without being subject to income tax that may be used to fund a retirement plan such as a traditional 401(k).

Provisional income—For income tax purposes, it is the amount of your income that is used to determine whether your Social Security benefits are subject to income tax. It includes certain income that is otherwise tax exempt.

Qualified Domestic Relations Order (QDRO)—Pronounced quad-row, this is a court order in a divorce that provides for the division and assignment of the interests in a qualified plan.

Qualified plan—A type of retirement plan set up by an employer that qualifies for special tax treatment under Section 401(a) of the Internal Revenue Code. A 401(k) is a qualified plan. An IRA is not, although it also receives special tax treatment.

QTIP trust—An acronym for Qualified Terminable Interest Property, this is a type of Marital Deduction Trust that provides income to a surviving spouse free of estate tax. Upon the death of the surviving spouse, the property passes to beneficiaries and is then potentially subject to estate tax.

REIT—An acronym for Real Estate Investment Trust, this is a mutual fund that invests in real estate.

Retirement Savings Contributions Credit—Also known as the Savers Credit, this is a tax credit that is available to lower-income individuals who contribute to an employer-sponsored retirement plan or an IRA.

Rollover—A tax-free distribution from one retirement plan to another retirement plan with a specific period of time as allowed by law. A common rollover occurs when someone leaves his job and rolls over his 401(k) account into an IRA.

Roth 401(k)—A type of 401(k) offered by an employer into which employees make after-tax contributions that grow tax free.

Roth IRA—A type of IRA in which contributions are made with after-tax money and grows tax free.

Self-Directed Brokerage window—A provision found in some 401(k) plans that enables employees participating in the plan to have the power to direct trades and invest in any stocks, bonds, and mutual funds they choose rather than have their investment choices limited to only those investment options listed specifically within the plan.

Self-Directed IRA—A type of IRA in which the owner of the account makes her own decisions as to the buying, selling, and holding of the investments that make up the IRA. Even in this situation, however, there must be a designated account custodian, such as a brokerage house, that holds the IRA.

SEP IRA—An acronym for Simplified Employee Pension Individual Retirement Account, this is a retirement program used primarily by self-employed people and owners of small businesses.

SIMPLE IRA or 401(K)—SIMPLE is an acronym for Savings Incentive Match Plan for Employees. (Pretty clever, eh?) This is a simplified type of a retirement plan that can utilize either the form of an IRA or a 401(k). Its use is limited to companies with fewer than 100 employees and is less costly than more conventional retirement plans.

Stretch IRA—A description of an IRA where, through the use of a properly worded beneficiary designation, the ability to extend tax-deferred growth with a traditional IRA or tax-free growth with a Roth IRA over many years and multiple generations is created.

Summary Plan Description (SPD)—A document that discloses all the important provisions in a company's qualified retirement plan, including fees, vesting requirements, and how benefits are determined.

Tax credit—A tax break that provides a dollar-for-dollar reduction in income tax liability.

Tax deduction—An amount subtracted from adjusted gross income to determine taxable income.

Tax-deferred growth—Occurs when the income taxes on the growth of money contributed on a tax-deductible basis to a retirement plan such as a traditional 401(k) or traditional IRA are deferred until money is withdrawn from the account.

Tax-free growth—Occurs when no income taxes are due on the value of the growth of money contributed to certain retirement plans, such as a Roth IRA or a Roth 401(k), into which contributions were made on an after-tax basis.

Traditional IRA—An IRA in which contributions are made on either a deductible or nondeductible basis and which grows on a tax-deferred basis.

Vesting—The period that an employee must work at a particular company before she has full rights and total access to the employer contributions to her account with an employer-sponsored retirement plan.

TRUTH

48

IRS Publication 590:
Worksheets and Tables

IRS Publication 590 contains a number of helpful tables and worksheets that can assist you in determining the minimum required distributions for beneficiaries and owners of IRAs and 401(k)s, as well as determine how Social Security benefits are affected by IRAs.

You can download PDFs of these tables and worksheets, which are contained in Appendixes A–C, from this book's Web site at www.ftpress.com/store/product.aspx?isbn=0132333848.

These appendixes are

- Appendix A: Summary Record of Traditional IRA(s) for 2007 and Worksheet for Determining Required Minimum Distributions

- Appendix B: Worksheets for Social Security Recipients Who Contribute to a Traditional IRA

- Appendix C: Life Expectancy Tables

About the Author

Steve Weisman is Senior Lecturer at Bentley College in the department of Law, Tax, and Financial Planning. He has also taught courses on financial planning at the University of Massachusetts, Curry College, and Boston University. He is a host on the nationally syndicated radio show "A Touch of Grey," heard on more than 50 stations, including NYC's legendary WABC and KRLA Los Angeles. A member of the National Association of Elder Law Attorneys, Steve is legal editor and a columnist for *Talkers Magazine* and writes for publications ranging from *The Boston Globe* to *US Air*. His books include *Boomer or Bust*, *The Truth About Avoiding Scams*, and *The Truth About Buying Annuities*. Weisman has earned a Certificate of Merit for legal journalism from the American Bar Association.

Acknowledgments

To my friends and colleagues at Bentley College, Joe Newpol, Steve Lichtenstein, Iris Berdrow, Aaron Nurick, Jack Lynch, Bill Wiggins, and Roseann Cotoni for their continuing support and encouragement.

Simply the best thinking

THE TRUTH AND NOTHING BUT THE TRUTH

The **Truth About** Series offers the collected and distilled knowledge on a topic and shows you how to apply this knowledge in your everyday life.

Arm yourself with everything you need for protection: the up-to-the-minute knowledge you need to sniff out even the subtlest, most well-crafted scams.

ISBN: 0132333856
Steve Weisman
$18.99

Create a long-term tax plan that could save you hundreds of thousands of dollars over your lifetime.

ISBN: 0137153864
S. Kay Bell
$18.99

Use this guide to pick the best annuities and avoid the ripoffs!

ISBN: 0132353083
Steve Weisman
$18.99